GLOBETROT

Wildlife Guide

COSTA RICA

NEW
HOLLAND

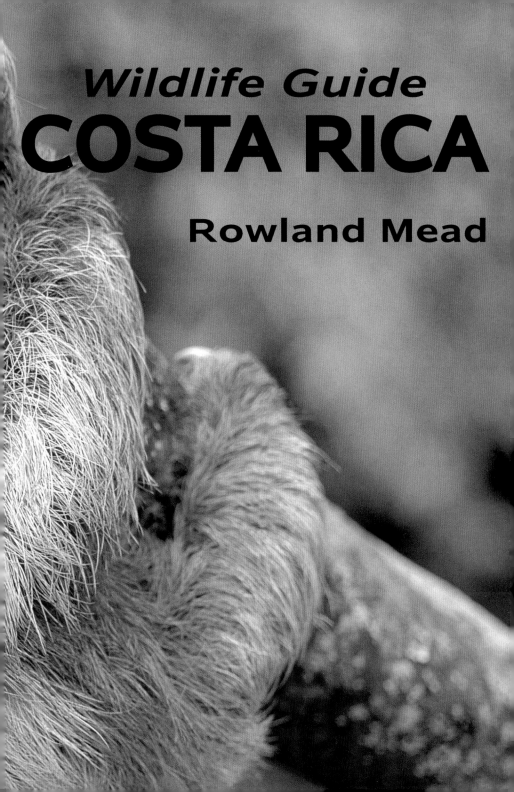

Wildlife Guide
COSTA RICA

Rowland Mead

CONTENTS

INTRODUCTION

Status of Costa Rican Wildlife

Located in the Central American Isthmus between Nicaragua and Panama, tiny Costa Rica, only a quarter the size of Scotland, packs an amazing diversity into its 51,120km² (19,739 sq miles). Its high mountain ranges, often volcanic, reaching 3820m (12,533ft) at Mt Chirripó, give rise to a variety of climate and vegetation zones. The Caribbean coast is hot and steamy and covered with lowland rainforest; in the west, the Pacific coast is drier, with cattle ranching predominating. Further south, the Pacific coast returns to rainforest. Inland, the Central Valley is surrounded by volcanoes, many benignly active. Their ash has weathered into a fertile soil ideal for the production of coffee, for many years the country's main export.

Endangered species are believed to be in imminent danger of extinction throughout their range and are unlikely to survive unless comprehensive conservation measures are taken.

Threatened species are thought to be undergoing rapid declines in their population and unless the reasons can be discovered and conservation measures taken, they are likely to be classified as endangered in the future.

Vulnerable species are likely to be threatened in the future for reasons such as habitat destruction.

Opposite, top to bottom:
Anhinga drying its wings on a log in the Tortuguero National Park; accommodation at the Lomas de Volcano Hotel with Arenal in the background; tourists on the path to Cuesta del Agua — rain protection is essential for hikers.

Introduction

Life Expectancy

The recent annual report of the World Health Organization showed that life expectancy for Costa Ricans is currently 77.02 years. This is one of the highest rates in the world, comparing favourably with neighbouring countries. The rate is the second highest in the Americas after Canada. The reasons for the high life expectancy are low infant mortality, low child mortality, good drinking water, adequate sewage disposal and close control of contagious illnesses. The agreeable climate of the Central Valley, where most *Ticos* live, plus the healthy diet, are other important factors.

Costa Rica has become one of the world's prime ecotourism destinations – helped by the fact that 27% of the countryside is protected to some degree. Activity holidays also have a big following, with scuba diving, hiking, surfing and big game fishing all highly popular.

Above all, however, tourists perceive Costa Rica to be safe. It has been a democracy for over 100 years and abolished its armed forces after the Civil War in 1948, remaining free of the coups and dictatorships that beleaguer neighbouring countries. In recognition of this, over 35,000 American citizens have settled here. The latest (2006) estimated population of Costa Rica is 4,075,261, around one tenth of whom live in San José, the capital. Catholicsm is the main religion and this is still a strongly family-orientated society. The Costa Ricans refer to themselves as *Ticos* and their warmth always leaves a lasting impression on visitors to this fascinating country.

THE BACKGROUND

Costa Rica owes its physical origin to the movement of tectonic plates in the earth's crust. In the recent geological past, part of the Pacific Plate moved against the Caribbean Plate, forming a 'collision zone' resulting in the upfolding of rocks into mountains and the outpouring of volcanic material. This eventually formed a land bridge or isthmus linking the continents of North and South America, a passage that was used by wildlife and eventually humans. Costa Rica remains on the plate boundary today and volcanoes and frequent earthquakes are typical of this unstable zone.

Some 60 volcanoes can be identified and of these eight have been recently active. They occur in four ranges, which run in a northeast-southwest direction from the Nicaraguan to the Panamanian border. In the northwest is the Cordillera de Guanacaste, with a string of volcanoes, including Volcán Orosí (1487m/4878ft), Volcán Santa María (1916m/6286ft) and Volcán Rincón de la Vieja (1895m/6217ft). Further southeast is the Cordillera de Tilarán, with the active Volcán Arenal (1633m/5358ft), and this mountain chain then merges into the Cordillera Central, with a number of volcanoes that can be seen from the capital San José. These include the accessible Volcán Poás (2704m/8871ft), Volcán Irazú

The Background

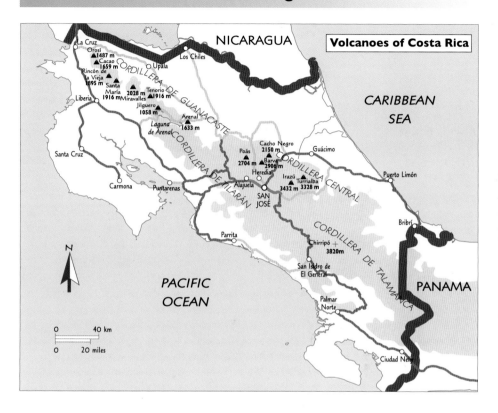

(3432m/11,260ft) and also Volcán Barva (2906m/9534ft). The fourth chain is the Cordillera de Talamanca. This huge granite batholith's uplift led to the formation of Costa Rica's highest mountain, Cerro Chirripó (3820m/12,533ft).

Within the mountain chains lies the Central Valley, in reality an undulating plateau at a height of between 1000m (3280ft) and 1500m (4920ft). The landscape here is formed of volcanic soil which, along with the amenable climate of the Central Valley, has led to the location here of four of the main cities of Costa Rica.

On either side of the highlands are coastal lowlands. To the east lie the Caribbean lowlands, a generally flat area crossed by rivers such as the Reventazón and the Chirripó. Much of the rainforest vegetation here has been cleared for agriculture.

Introduction

The Pacific lowlands, on the other hand, are more undulating. The pronounced dry season produces savannah and dry tropical forest land, on which cattle ranching thrives. Numerous rivers flow west off the Cordilleras, such as the Río Tempisque in the north, flowing into the gulf of Nicoya. Further south, the main river is the Térraba, which forms a delta in the Bay of Coronado.

The Pacific and Caribbean coastlines present marked contrasts. The Caribbean coast is short, stretching for little over 200km (125 miles), and is characterized by sandy beaches, backed by mangroves and rainforest. Offshore, particularly in the south, are occasional coral reefs, but many of these have been destroyed as recent earth movements have raised their levels. An intracoastal waterway runs parallel to the shore in the north, providing local people with their main form of communication.

The Pacific coast, in contrast, stretches for over 1000km (620 miles) and is generally rugged, with headlands interspersed with mangroves and sandy beaches. There are two important peninsulas running parallel to the coast. In the north, the Peninsula de Nicoya is backed by the Gulf of Nicoya, while in the south the Osa Peninsula protects the Golfo Dulce. The combination of a favourable climate and attractive scenery has led to the development of a thriving tourist industry on the Pacific coast.

Climate

An understanding of the climate of Costa Rica is important for the ecotourist, who would need to know what time of year to visit and which areas are best according to the season, region and altitude. As a subtropical country, Costa Rica experiences two seasons. The dry season lasts from December to April and is known as *verano* (summer), while the remainder of the year comprises the wet season, called *invierno* (winter). Some areas of the country experience a short dry spell between July and September, known as *veranillo* (little summer). All this, of course, is a simplification because there are considerable differences depending on position and altitude. The Caribbean lowlands, for example, receive rain throughout the year, often recording over 5000mm (200 in), a pattern repeated in the southern Pacific region, although the rainfall figures there are lower. The hottest

Costa Rica's Growing Population

The country's population has now topped the four million mark. The startling recent increase has not been caused by a significant rise in the birth rate or longer life expectancy, but by the growth in immigration. While many North Americans have chosen to live in Costa Rica, the majority of immigrants have come from other Central American countries, particularly neighbouring Nicaragua, which has a staggering 50% unemployment rate. Other nicas (Nicaraguans) fled the country after the drought caused by el Niño and the devastation wrecked by Hurricane Mitch in 1998. By and large, Costa Rica, with its healthy economy, has absorbed these immigrants without too many problems.

and driest part of the country is Guanacaste province in the northwest, where temperatures often reach 40°C (104°F), while the coldest area is the peak of Chirripó, which often experiences temperatures below freezing point. The most agreeable climate to be found in Costa Rica is in the Central Valley, where temperatures average a healthy 20°C (68°F) throughout the year.

The higher peaks of the Cordilleras are often cloud-covered and tourists visiting the most popular volcanoes, such as Poás and Irazú, should do so early in the morning before the mists descend. The dry season is the peak period for tourism, both for foreigners and Costa Ricans. Accommodation charges are highest at this time and advance booking for hotels is recommended. However, the tourist authorities in Costa Rica are trying hard to extend the tourist year by referring to the wet season as the Green Season. Certainly, it does not rain all the time and mornings can often be dry. The resorts will not be crowded, but in some parts of the country access may be limited because of flooded roads, rivers and landslides. A 4WD vehicle is essential when travelling at this time of the year.

HABITATS

The Holdridge Classification

In 1947, the biologist L H Holdridge devised a system of classifying vegetation zones based on rainfall, temperature and season, with each zone possessing a typical natural vegetation. Twelve zones have been identified in Costa Rica, ranging from sea level mangrove swamps to alpine páramo.

Costa Rica has a wide spread of tropical forest, which can be divided into three broad sections:

Tropical Lowland Rainforest

Found in the Caribbean lowlands and the south Pacific lowlands, these are the classic tropical forests. They appear to be stratified and they are typified by a canopy, above which soar tall evergreen trees, which may reach a height of over 50m (165ft). One of the tallest trees of the forest is the kapok, whose seeds are often used to stuff cushions and furniture. Beneath this is a sub-canopy or understorey, while at ground level there is either a shrub layer

Education in Costa Rica

It is claimed that 25% of the national budget goes into education. In fact, education in Costa Rica has been compulsory since 1869 and students must attend school until the end of the ninth grade, which is at the age of 14–15. As a result the country has the highest literacy rate in Latin America (93%). Large numbers of urban children go to pre-school classes. There are 3442 primary schools and about 200 secondary schools. The higher education sector is strong, with six universities. The main problem concerns the lack of convenient schools in remote areas of the country, particularly at secondary level.

Introduction

Costa Rica's national flag consists of five vertical stripes, coloured blue, white, red, white and blue. *Ticos* will explain that the blue represents the sky and the sea, the white stands for peace with their neighbours to the north and south, while the red represents the blood lost in achieving democracy.

or it will be largely bare, depending on the density of the canopy and the amount of sunlight that can penetrate. The larger trees have huge buttress roots, which provide a support for the tree, compensating for the shallow root system. Typical plants of the rainforest include palms, vines and lianas, and epiphytes such as orchids and bromeliads. A striking feature of the rainforest is the wide variety of plants found within a small area – it is not unknown to find up to 100 tree species per acre.

Tropical Lowland Dry Forest

Less species-rich than the rainforest, the dry forest is typified by deciduous trees, which lose their leaves during the dry season. Buttressing is also less common. Because of the sparser canopy the shrub layer is dense. Vines are found, but epiphytes are rare. The lowland dry forest in Costa Rica is confined to the northern

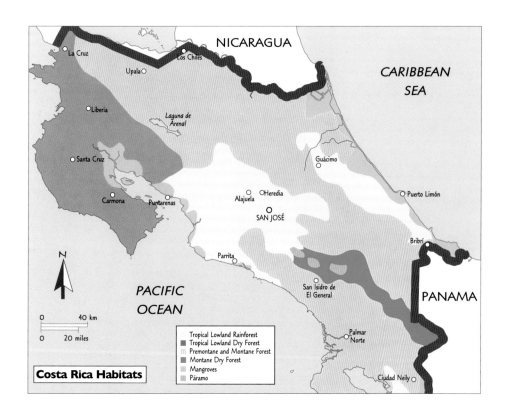

NICARAGUA

La Cruz
Los Chiles
Upala

CARIBBEAN SEA

Liberia
Laguna de Arenal

Santa Cruz

Guácimo

Carmona
Puntarenas
Alajuela
Heredia
SAN JOSÉ
Puerto Limón

Bribri

N

Parrita

PACIFIC OCEAN

San Isidro de El General

PANAMA

0   40 km
0   20 miles

Tropical Lowland Rainforest
Tropical Lowland Dry Forest
Premontane and Montane Forest
Montane Dry Forest
Mangroves
Páramo

Palmar Norte

Ciudad Neily

Costa Rica Habitats

Habitats

Pacific lowlands north of Puntarenas. The dry forest areas make excellent agricultural land and are easily cleared by fire, so that only a few protected areas remain.

Premontane and Montane Forest

Often referred to as Highland and Cloud Forest, these habitats occur at higher elevations along Costa Rica's mountain ranges. They are mixed deciduous and evergreen at lower levels, but progressively more evergreen with altitude. Buttressing, too, reduces with altitude. Epiphytes and vines are common. The climate is cooler and less humid than in the lowland forests. Mists of cloud or fog cover the canopy for much of the time and the forests drip with water that has condensed out of the atmosphere. The cloud forests have fewer species than those at lower levels, but often have more endemic species.

Below: Forest vegetation on the slopes of Volcán Arenal.

Mangroves

Found at the junction of land and sea, this habitat is valuable in the fight against tidal erosion and reclaiming land from the ocean. There are five species of mangrove in Costa Rica and these shrubby trees are notable for their interlocking aerial roots. Mangrove trees are halophytes (can be found in brackish water and will tolerate salty conditions) but in actual fact they grow better in fresh water. They spread quickly, their seeds falling down into the mud at low tide and putting down roots immediately.

Mangrove swamps are found along both the Caribbean and Pacific coasts wherever there are tidal estuaries.

Páramo

This habitat occurs above the treeline at the highest levels in Costa Rica, mainly around the summit of Chirripó, the country's highest mountain. It consists of subalpine grasses and shrubs in often boggy conditions.

Introduction

Wildlife Classification or Taxonomy

The example of the Brown Pelican:

Kingdom: Animalia

Phylum: Chordata,

Subphylum Vertebrata

Class: Aves (birds)

Order: Pelicaniformes (also includes Boobies and Frigatebirds)

Family: Pelicanidae

Genus: *Pelicanus*

Species: *Pelicanus occidentalis*; Brown Pelican, Pelicano Moreno.

THE WILDLIFE

Firstly, do not expect to see big game in Costa Rica – no lions, leopards, wildebeest or elephants. What you will see, however, is a tremendous biodiversity for such a small country. The reasons are clear. Costa Rica is part of a narrow land ridge between North and South America and therefore has species from both continents. The variety in climate and altitude adds to this a large number of life zones, producing a variety of habitats. The statistics are astounding: some 10,000 species of plants have been recorded in Costa Rica, including 1200 types of orchid; over 1400 species of tree have been noted, many in the rainforests, where it is possible to identify 200 types in one acre; there are 250 species of mammals, half of which are bats; 870 species of birds have been spotted, including many rarities, making Costa Rica a Mecca for bird-watchers; there are 120 types of frogs and toads, including tree frogs and poison dart frogs; there are 127 species of snakes, many of them extremely venomous although fortunately rarely seen; 130 species of freshwater fish have been recorded; 360,000 insects have been noted, including 10% of the world's butterflies; finally, there are four species of sea turtle nesting on Costa Rica's beaches – enough statistics to attract and satisfy any keen ecotourist.

Mammals

All visitors to the rainforests of Costa Rica hope to spot the wildcats, such as the Jaguar, Puma, Ocelot, Jaguarundi and Margay. They will usually be disappointed, however, as these felines are nocturnal, elusive and rarely seen. The same applies to the pig-like Tapir, a distant relative of the rhinoceros with a prehensile snout, and which can weigh up to 300kg (660 lb). Costa Rica has four of the 70-odd monkeys that are found in the New World. Three of these are quite common. The largely black Howler Monkey is the most likely to be seen and heard as its voice is one of the loudest in the animal world. The White-faced Capuchin Monkey is also widely found in wet and dry forests and even mangroves. The Spider Monkey is the most elegant of the primates, using its prehensile tail as a fifth limb as it swings acrobatically through the forest. The rarest in this class is the delightful little Squirrel Monkey, which is found only in Costa Rica and Panama and is in danger of extinction. Small groups can be found in the Osa Peninsula and Manuel Antonio National Park.

The Wildlife

Expertly camouflaged in the rainforests are the slow-moving sloths, of which there are two types in Costa Rica: the Three-toed Sloth, active by day, and the largely nocturnal Two-toed Sloth. The sloths' main predators are eagles, but they are most at risk when they descend, once a week, to the forest floor to defecate.

Other interesting mammals include the anteaters, of which there are three local varieties. They are unique in that they have no teeth, but use a long sticky tongue to take in their main diet of ants and termites. They are related to the armadillos, of which there are two types in Costa Rica, having migrated from the South American continent. They are unusual in that their bodies have bands of pliable protective plates, allowing them to curl up in a ball when threatened.

Costa Rica has nine species of marsupials. The most likely to be encountered is the Common Opossum, which often lives near human habitations and forages in rubbish dumps. There are six species of raccoon in the country, of which the Coati is the most commonly seen, the other five being nocturnal. Coatis have a long ringed tail which is often held vertically when it is on the move. The pig-like Peccaries travel in groups through the forest, foraging for roots, fruit and seeds. They have been known to be aggressive to hikers.

There are around 50 rodent species in Costa Rica. Often seen in the dry forest areas is the reddish brown Agouti, which looks rather like a long-legged guinea pig. Of the five squirrel species in the country, the Red-tailed and the Variegated are the most likely to be seen. The Red-tailed is a denizen of the wet forest areas, while the beautifully marked Variegated Squirrel is more likely to found in drier areas, often close to human habitation.

Below: A White-faced Capuchin Monkey photographed in the Manuel Antonio National Park, where they scavenge along the beaches and can be a nuisance to visitors.

Introduction

Finally there are the deer. There are two varieties in Costa Rica. The White-tailed Deer is the more common and larger of the two and is found in open drier forests, while the Red Brocket Deer prefers denser, wet forest. Both feed on grass and leaves. Deer are preyed upon by the larger cats, such as the jaguar and the puma.

Amphibians and Reptiles

Costa Rica boasts many brightly coloured frogs and toads, particularly in the rainforests; many no bigger than a thumbnail. There are several varieties of poison dart frogs, but there is no evidence that their toxic secretions were ever used by the indigenous people of the country to tip their darts for hunting. The rainforest waterways are often the haunt of Caimans and crocodiles, though these rarely reach a size that makes them dangerous to man. A remarkable amphibian is the Basilisk or Jesus Christ lizard, which patters over the water when disturbed. The most widespread lizard is the iguana, of which there are a number of species, some even being found in hotel grounds where they can become very tame. Some iguana farms have been set up in order to breed iguanas to return to the wild or for their meat.

Right: Among Costa Rica's 127 species of snake, the Coral Snake is one of the most attractive.

The Wildlife

Costa Rica has five species of sea turtle – the Olive Ridley, Loggerhead, Hawksbill, Green and the huge Leatherback. They nest on a number of beaches on both shores of the country, when they come ashore in large numbers, an event known as an *arribada*. In addition there are freshwater turtles in the rivers and mangrove swamps. Of Costa Rica's 127 species of snake, 22 are venomous, including the Bushmaster (the largest in the New World), the aggressive Fer-de-lance and the small Eyelash Viper. It should be stressed, however, that the vast majority of the country's snakes are non-venomous and that those that are venomous are largely nocturnal and rarely seen.

Insects

Few visitors will fail to be impressed by Costa Rica's butterflies. Some 10% of the world's total may be seen here, including the stunning Blue Morpho, which can measure 20cm (8in) across. It makes a marvellous sight as it glides through rainforest clearings. Other colourful butterflies include the Orange-barred Sulphur, Giant Swallowtail, Zebra Longwing and Owl Butterfly. Less welcome are mosquitoes, which inhabit the wetter, humid areas. There are many species of ants. On the forest floor, the Leaf-cutter Ants are always busy, carrying pieces of leaf along trails to their nests. The larger Bullet Ants, however, should be avoided, as their bite can be painful.

Birds

Costa Rica has become one of the world's most exciting destinations for bird-watching. Including migratory birds, an incredible 870 species have been recorded, comprising many exotic and rare examples. The bird that most foreign enthusiasts hope to see is the Resplendent Quetzal. Highly regarded by the Maya and the Aztecs, its long tail feathers were used both in headdresses and as currency. Today, this brightly coloured bird is becoming increasingly rare, but can still be seen at Monteverde and on the Osa Peninsula. Other exotic (and noisy) birds include the Scarlet Macaw, toucans and a whole range of parrots and parakeets. Hummingbirds are one of the most common bird varieties in Costa Rica and can often be seen enjoying nectar from flowers while hovering. There are some 50 species of hummingbird in the country and a number migrate to North

Introduction

OTS – The Organization for Tropical Studies

This organization was set up by a group of American universities who were looking for a base to support their faculty research and to train graduate students in tropical biology. It maintains three research stations in Costa Rica – La Selva, Palo Verde and Las Cruces (which includes the Wilson Botanical Garden) – where students can study tropical ecology, agriculture, conservation biology and many more topics. The research stations welcome visitors and can provide guides for tours around their extensive grounds. Visit www.ots.duke.edu for more information.

America for the northern summer. Numerous songbirds, such as tanagers and flycatchers, follow the same route. Water and wetland birds are easily observed and identified and include spoonbills, herons, egrets, storks and anhingas. The most common shorebirds are Brown Pelicans, Brown Boobys, Magnificent Frigatebirds, Laughing Gulls and Royal Terns, along with scores of migratory waders, such as the Spotted Sandpiper and the Willet.

Amongst the raptors, the most likely ones to be noticed are the Black Hawk, the Broad-winged Hawk and the aptly named Laughing Falcon. Ospreys are still common along the rainforest waterways. Many examples of the flycatcher family can be seen on roadside wires, including the easily identified Scissor-tailed Flycatcher and the attractive Kiskadee, with its onomatopoeic song. Some birds are extremely common, such as the Great-tailed Grackle and the Bronzed Cowbird, which are often seen in flocks.

A spectacular sight is the Montezuma's Oropendula, whose colonial nests festoon trees. Finally, one of the most widespread species of bird in Costa Rica is the vulture, seen either as a reeling speck in the sky or waiting hopefully on a roadside for a squashed animal. Of the three vulture species, the Black Vulture is the most common. Needless to say, a good bird identification guide is essential.

THE NATIONAL PARKS SYSTEM

From the end of World War II to the 1970s, Costa Rica followed a policy of stripping its forests for agriculture. Indeed, had the rate of deforestation continued there would have been no trees left by the 21st century. Fortunately the authorities began to realize that they were in danger of losing something special and in 1970, spurred on by a number of dedicated individuals and the Organization for Tropical Studies, they set up the National Parks Service. The policy now was to move away from state-sponsored clearance of land for agriculture to protecting valuable habitats for posterity. In 1995, a further reorganization set up eleven regions forming the National System of Protected Areas (SINAC, or Sistema Nacional de Areas de Conservación), which is administered by the Ministry for Environment and Energy (MINAE, or Ministerio del Ambiente y Energía). In addition to the

The National Parks System

Left: *The attractive Kiskadee is widespread throughout Costa Rica, frequenting gardens and clearings up to 1800m (6000ft). It is noted for its onomatopoeic three-note call.*

26 national parks, the ministry protects a number of forest and biological reserves, wildlife refuges and archaeological sites, amounting to over a quarter of the country. With the addition of a number of private reserves and research stations, the amount of protected land in Costa Rica is close on 27% of the country. These areas are estimated to protect 75% of Costa Rica's flora and fauna, while they also protect the watersheds that feed the country's hydroelectric systems.

So popular have the parks been (at present around 300,000 foreign visitors annually visit them) that some of the most visited reserves have started to show some wear and tear. Management policies have had to be introduced and limits have been set on the number of visitors allowed at any one time, while some parks close for one day a week. Admission fees, if charged at all, were quite low in the early days, but in 1994 they were increased dramatically. The money raised has helped to set up ranger stations, buy vehicles and equipment for the rangers, maintain hiking trails and sponsor research. There is a standard entrance fee (US$7 at the time of writing) to the national parks and, in theory, it is perfectly possible to pay on arrival at the entrance to the park, but if you wish to visit one of the more popular parks, such as Manuel Antonio, it might be prudent to book in advance from the Fundación de Parques Nacionales, tel: 2257 2239 or www.minae.go.cr

Introduction

Time Difference

Costa Rica is six hours behind GMT, the same as Central time in the USA. Remember that there is no daylight saving time alteration, so that it gets dark early – around 18:00 throughout the year.

PLANNING YOUR TRIP
When to Go

Most visitors to Costa Rica will wish to go to the country during the dry season, which lasts from December to April. During this time, the Central Valley and the north and central Pacific coasts will be virtually rain-free and hot. Bear in mind, however, that Christmas, New Year and Easter are peak periods when the *Ticos* also take their holidays and hotels and rental cars may well be fully booked. The rainy season is between May and November, but even during this period the mornings can often be sunny. The Caribbean slope and the southwest Pacific coast receive rain throughout the year. The tourist authorities in Costa Rica have renamed the wet season as the 'green season' and this does have its attractions as the countryside is fresh and discounts are often available at hotels. Be aware, however, that some accommodation may close for renovation during the wet season. Another problem is that some roads may be inaccessible due to flooding and a 4WD vehicle is advisable at this time of the year.

What to Pack

A general rule is to travel light. Lay out everything you might want to take and then cut it by half! Don't take anything of value that you cannot afford to lose. Limit your changes of clothing by taking items that can be washed and will dry overnight. 'Safari jackets' with a range of pockets are very useful, while trousers that unzip above the knee to become shorts are very versatile. Remember to cater for changes of temperature, from the humidity of the rainforests to the chill of mountain tops – this applies to footwear also. Rubber boots are the most practical items on muddy rainforest trails, although these are often provided by lodges. Always be prepared for rain, particularly in the wet season. Ponchos are popular and a fold-up umbrella, although it may look ridiculous, is a handy item. A sunhat is advisable if you are visiting the hotter, drier parts of the country. Equipment is often provided for snorkelling, but you might wish to take your own mask. Evening wear should be casual but smart. If you take medication, make sure that you have sufficient supplies to last the holiday. The case versus rucksack argument will depend on the nature of your tour. If your trip is organized by a tour operator, a case with a small day-rucksack will be ideal. If

The Ecotourist's First-aid Kit

• **Sun block** – Costa Rica's heat can seem searing, especially if you have come directly from a northern winter.
• **After sun cream** – preferably use a cream which also contains an insect deterrent.
• **Calamine lotion** – for treating sunburn and insect bites.
• **Imodium** – probably the best treatment for diarrhoea.
• **Rehydration sachets.**
• Assorted **bandages** and **plasters.**
• **Sulphur powder** for protection against sand fleas.

Planning Your Trip

you are travelling independently and are planning hikes, then a rucksack is essential. Bear in mind, however, that it is possible to leave items in the storerooms of hotels in San José and collect them again on your return.

Getting There

Costa Rica can be reached by air, land and water.

By Air

Numerous US airlines, such as Continental, American and Delta, run daily scheduled flights from a number of American airports to Costa Rica. At the time of writing there are no direct scheduled flights from the UK to Costa Rica, so at least one stopover must be made. However, First Choice run direct flights from London Gatwick to service their package holidays and it may be possible to obtain seats on a 'flight only' basis. Bear in mind that these flights only run from May to October, which is, of course, the wet season in Costa Rica. One route could be to Madrid and then onward with Iberia directly to San José. An alternative would be to fly with BA to Miami or Houston and then continue to San José with an American airline. The main point of entry is San José's Juan Santamaría Airport, a 16km (10-mile) drive from the city centre. Juan Santamaría is a modern, user-friendly airport with a particularly pleasant departure lounge – remember to keep back some dollars for the departure tax. A taxi ride to the city centre takes about 20 minutes and the fare is paid at a kiosk, not to the driver. A new international airport has been opened at Liberia in the northwest of the country, mainly catering for US charter flights to the holiday resorts on the Pacific coast.

By Road

It is possible for US citizens to drive to Costa Rica, but this is not a popular option. It is 4000km (2500 miles) from the US border to San José through several countries, many regarded as unsafe, while border delays can be expected and the paperwork is challenging. Buses run to San José from Panama City in Panama and Managua in Nicaragua. Services are run by two companies: **Tica Bus**, tel: (506) 2221 8954 and **Sirca**, tel: (506) 2222 5541.

Practical Packing Essentials

Penknife
Universal sink plug
Torch
Address book
Notebook
Electrical adapter
String or cord (to act as a washing line)
Travel alarm clock
First-aid kit
Water bottle
Toilet paper
Contraceptives

Introduction

The *Ticos*

The strange word *Tico* is in fact the name commonly used to refer to the inhabitants of Costa Rica. In Spanish, the diminutive is formed by dropping the final 'a' or 'o' of a word and adding 'ita' or 'ito' depending on the gender, as a way of being friendly and familiar. For example, an *amigo*, or friend, who was particularly close might be referred to as an *amiguito*. Costa Rica has been somewhat isolated over the centuries and the language developed its own idiosyncrasies, one of which was to use *ico* as a diminutive. For example, whereas in Castilian Spanish the diminutive of *poco* (little or few) would be *poquito*, the Costa Ricans would use *poquitico*. As a result, Costa Ricans have always fondly been called *Ticos*. Although these days the correct grammatical use of the diminutive is taught and understood in schools, the name *Tico* survives.

By Sea

A considerable number of cruise ships visit Costa Rica during the dry season, usually calling at Puerto Limón on the Caribbean coast or Puerto Caldera on the Pacific side of the country. For many people, this will be their first experience of Costa Rica and they will find that although the cruise lines rarely stay for more than 24 hours, they provide plenty of excursions of an ecological nature. From Puerto Limón, for example, day tours are offered to the Tortuguero Channels and the Rainforest Aerial Tram, while from Puerto Caldera it is possible to visit both the Carrera and Manuel Antonio national parks.

Entry Requirements

Citizens of the United States, Canada and Panama are allowed to enter Costa Rica with a tourist card plus one other piece of identification, but since a passport might be required for other transactions, it is probably best to take one with you anyway. A passport is required for all other visitors. Citizens of the USA, UK, Japan, Canada and most EU countries are granted a 90-day entry stamp. Citizens of Australia and New Zealand are allowed to stay in Costa Rica for 30 days. Most other nationalities require a visa, which should be obtained from Costa Rican consulates before travelling. Visitors wishing to stay for longer can apply for an extension, but as this can be a time-consuming process, it is often more convenient to leave the country for 72 hours by crossing the border into Nicaragua or Panama and then obtain a re-entry stamp.

Customs

Visitors to Costa Rica are allowed to bring in 3 litres of wine or spirits, 500 cigarettes (or 500g of tobacco) and six rolls of film (although this is rarely checked as most people now use digital cameras). Prescription drugs should be kept in their original containers. There is usually no problem with sporting gear and other equipment.

Health Considerations

Although vaccinations are not mandatory for Costa Rica, it is wise to make sure that your polio, tetanus, typhoid and hepatitis jabs are up to date before setting off. There is a slight risk of malaria in the lowland rainforest areas of the country. Many visitors, however, might prefer not to take a course of expensive anti-malarial drugs, with possibly unpleasant side effects. In that case, take the usual precautions against being bitten, particularly at night. There have also been cases of dengue fever, and the best advice is to avoid being bitten by using a good insect repellent and covering up, particularly at night. For current advice on health matters consult the World Health Organization's website: www.who.int

Sanitary standards in Costa Rica are high and your chances of becoming ill are low, but if the worst happens you can be reassured that the country has an efficient health care system, with English-speaking doctors in most hospitals and clinics. Nevertheless, a good private medical insurance is highly recommended – in fact, most tour operators make this a requirement. Should you have a medical emergency, call 911.

Getting Around
By Road
Costa Rica's road system has improved considerably in recent years, but away from the main routes and towns, the road surfaces deteriorate, with king-sized potholes and gravel surfaces, and drivers often weave all over the road to avoid problems. In San José, a car is a dubious asset, owing to the grid-locked streets, one-way systems and theft from cars. In the more remote areas, signposting may be non-existent. Despite these problems, car hire is a popular choice for the independent traveller, providing freedom of movement and the ability to stop and deviate if something of interest turns up. The type of vehicle chosen will depend on the time of year and where you want go. In remote parts of the country, and especially during the wet season, a 4WD vehicle is essential. If you do decide to hire a car, familiarize yourself with the rules and regulations. In urban areas the speed limit is 40kph, with 80kph elsewhere. Wearing a seat belt is mandatory. Driving under the influence of drugs or alcohol is strictly prohibited. If you are involved in an accident, do not move the vehicle until a police officer has arrived. Police officers are not allowed to fine you on the spot or to remove any of your documents, but you must pull over if requested.

Car Hire Firms

Most international car hire firms have offices at the airport and in central San José, generally clustering along Paseo Colón:

Alamo, Av 18 C 11–13, north side of Plaza Gonzalez Viques, tel: 2233 7733, www.alamocostarica.com

Budget, C30, Paseo Colón, tel: 2223 3284, www.budget.co.cr

Hertz, C38, Paseo Colón, tel: 2221 1818, www.costaricarentacar.net

Europcar, C 36–38, Paseo Colón, tel: 2440 9990, www.europcar.co.cr

An alternative to hiring a car is to hire a private tour driver, who is English-speaking and who is familiar with the road system. Many local tour operators can provide this service, providing a driver who is also a wildlife guide.

Introduction

Bus Travel

Travel by public bus is a very popular and cheap way of getting around the country. Buses tend to leave on time and the service is reliable, particularly in the dry season. The main bus station in San José is the Coca Cola Terminal. The ICT office in San José can provide an up-to-date timetable.

Taxis

In San José, taxis are numerous and cheap. They are red, with a yellow triangle on the door. Make sure that the meter (*maria*) is switched on at the start of the journey. If you are part of a small group, taxis can be a surprisingly cheap way of putting together a tour.

Air Travel

Because of the time it takes to reach the more remote parts of the country by road, air travel is an alternative worth considering. Domestic routes are covered by two companies: **SANSA** (tel: 2221 9414, www.flysansa.com) uses the domestic terminal at Juan Santamaría airport. It is worth looking at their Costa Rica Airpass, which offers unlimited travel for periods of one week and two weeks. **NatureAir** (tel: 2220 3054, www.natureair.com) flies from Tobias Bolaños Airport at Pavos, 5km (3 miles) west of San José.

Domestic destinations include Barra del Colorado, Drake Bay, Golfito, Liberia, Nosara, Palmar Sur, Puerto Jiménez, Quepos, Sámara, Tamarindo, Tambor and Tortuguero.

Package Tours

The majority of visitors to Costa Rica use a package tour. This is a stress-free way to see the country, with transport arranged,

Below: The leafy grounds of Laguna Lodge, one of several lodges in the Tortuguero National Park. The lodges provide a variety of accommodation choices, varying from basic to luxurious, while their grounds are often full of birds and butterflies.

Planning Your Trip

hotels booked and a guide to provide information and solve any difficulties. For ecotourists, the guides provided are invariably excellent, often with a wide knowledge of the country's wildlife.

Accommodation

Visitors will find the full range of accommodation available in Costa Rica, from rustic homestays to top-class international hotels. When planning an independent trip, it is important to book ahead, particularly during the dry season and especially at Christmas, New Year and Easter. During the 'green season', there may be discounts of as much as 50%. It is important to have the booking confirmed, so that you know that the hotel has taken your enquiry seriously.

Hotels

A feature of recent years has been the growth of chains, such as Best Western, Meliá, Marriott and Barcelo, all of which have several hotels in the country. The Costa Rican Hotel Association (tel: 2248 0990, www.costaricanhotels.com) is a good source of information. There are numerous small 'boutique' hotels that can be highly recommended and some of them have grouped together to form a marketing consortium, the Small Distinctive Hotels of Costa Rica (tel: 2258 0150, www.distinctivehotels.com). Remember that hotels charge a 16% tax (13% sales tax and 3% room tax), which may not figure on your quote, while some hotels may add an additional 5–6% for paying by credit card.

Below the hotel classification comes accommodation with names such as *hostales, hospejades, pensiones* and *posadas*. At the budget end of the market the are *cabinas*, appealing mainly to *Tico* families at the weekends, but some set out to attract backpackers, who should log on to www.costarica.backpackers.com for information. There is a small network of youth hostels – 23 are affiliated to International Hostelling (www.youth-hostels-in.com/costarica). One of the more interesting developments in tourism in Costa Rica over the last 20 years has been the growth of establishments offering bed and breakfast. Some are traditional inns, more often they are houses of character converted by expats, but some Costa Rican families are now offering bed and breakfast – a good way of getting to know *Ticos* in their home environment.

Some Recommended Hotels in and around San José

Grano de Oro, C30 Av 2–4, San José, tel: 2255 3322, www.hotel granodeoro.com Delightful city centre hotel in an early 20th-century mansion with great attention to detail. Luxuriant patio garden.

Crowne Plaza Hotel San José Corobicí, Sabana Norte, San José, tel: 2232 8122 www.ichotelsgroup.com Large hotel with striking architecture on the corner of Parque Sábana. Pool, gym and casino. Popular with business people and tourists alike.

Ramada Plaza Herradura, close to the airport, reservations tel: 2209 9841, www.ramadaherradura.com Has 234 rooms with all facilities, some with Jacuzzis. It also has a number of restaurants, including authentic Japanese.

Hemingway Inn, C9 Av 9, San José, tel: 2257 8630, www.hemingwayinn.com Based in a colonial house in the stylish Amón district. Numerous references and photographs of the famous American author.

Introduction

Where to Go

Most organized tours start in Costa Rica's capital city, San José. Although ecotourists will be impatient to get out into the countryside and the national parks, it is well worth spending a day or two in San José. Don't expect any ancient monuments – they have all been felled by earthquakes – but there are some fascinating places to visit. Founded in 1737, San José was slow to develop and it was not until the wealth provided by coffee that it began to take on the trappings of a capital city. Today, it has a North American flavour, with a grid street pattern, a filigree of overhead power lines, neon signs and fast-food outlets, but amidst this rather uninspiring scene are some absolute gems. Don't miss the National Theatre. It was built in the 1890s after the opera singer, Adelina Patti, refused to perform in Costa Rica, claiming that there was no suitable venue. After this snub, the coffee barons soon raised the money to build a theatre, employing craftsmen from all over Europe. The building is resplendent with marble, gilding, hardwood and glasswork, and well worth a visit.

Also not to be missed is the National Museum, housed in the old Bellavista army barracks – be sure to look at the south wall, pock marked from bullets dating from the 1948 Civil War. Inside is a superb archaeology section, with many artefacts from the pre-Columbian era, and a section detailing the racial and ethnic origins of present-day Costa Ricans. Outside is a collection of some of Costa Rica's common trees and shrubs, a herb garden and an informative butterfly garden. There are also a number of other museums, mostly housed in unlikely places.

Day Trips

Staying in San José for a few days has other advantages in that it makes an excellent base for day trips to nearby locations. The craft village of Sarchí is within easy reach and the coffee plantation of Café Britt is a popular excursion. The volcanoes of Poás and Irazú are quite accessible and one of these should feature on every tourist's itinerary. The Lankester Botanical Gardens, with its exotic collection of orchids and attendant butterflies, will give hints of the pleasures to come, while the Rainforest Aerial Tram is a mere 20km (12 miles) from San José and gives a wonderful introduction to the rainforest canopy. Also within easy reach is

Planning Your Trip

Left: Whitewater rafting is a popular adventure activity in Costa Rica. Here, a rafting group paddle a calm section of the Corobicí River before tackling the rapids.

the attractive Orosí Valley, at the end of which is the little visited Tapanti National Park, whose rainforest is bursting with wildlife.

Two- and Three-day Tours from San José

One of the most popular three-day tours from San José is to the Tortuguero National Park, passing through banana plantations and Braulio Carrillo National Park en route. Launches take visitors on a two-hour journey along rainforest channels to lodges at Tortuguero village for a two-night stay. Guided walks and boat trips are on offer, while kayaks can be hired for gentle paddles around the creeks.

Another attractive three-day option is to the Monteverde area. With two nights' accommodation, there is the opportunity to visit the main Cloud Forest Reserve, plus the Santa Elena Reserve and the Childrens' Eternal Rain Forest. Three days is also enough time to stay over at Manuel Antonio, Costa Rica's most popular national park, and have the opportunity of seeing the squirrel

Introduction

Activity Times of Animals

Nocturnal animals are active at night. Diurnal animals are active during the day. Crepuscular animals are active at dusk and dawn.

monkey, the rarest of the country's primates. To spend three days in the extreme south of the Pacific coast in the Osa Peninsula and Corcovado National Park requires flying to and from Golfito or Drake Bay, but it is well worth the extra expense for a pristine rainforest experience.

One-week Tours

A number of companies run seven-day tours starting with a day in San José, visiting the city's main sights in the morning followed by an afternoon in the Orosí Valley taking in the Lankester Gardens. Then follows a three-day tour to the Tortuguero National Park, with two nights in a jungle lodge. The tour continues to the north of the country to the area around Arenal, Costa Rica's most active volcano, taking in canopy tours and bathing in hot springs. The one-week tour concludes in San José after stopping off at one of the other volcanoes, such as Poás, or visiting a coffee plantation or a butterfly farm.

Ten- and Fourteen-day Tours

These can include any combination of the above, plus other reserves and parks, such as Cahuita, Barra del Colorado, and Carrera. Many local tour operators can provide tailor-made itineraries for small groups, depending on the interests of the members, also arranging accommodation and providing transport between locations.

Pacific Coast Extensions

The northern and central Pacific coast has Costa Rica's driest and warmest climate and after a hard week's hiking or bird-watching, many travellers find the idea of chilling out on the beach an attractive option. The most popular resort on the Guanacaste coast is Tamarindo, where surfing, snorkelling and turtle-watching are available. Further down the coast, Sámara and Nosara are other popular resorts. In the extreme south of the Nicoya Peninsula, Montezuma appeals to the backpacking crowd, while further east, the delightful Tango Mar and the massive Playa Tambor have their devotees. Despite the attractions of the beach, all of these resorts are within reasonable distance of national parks and reserves. From Tamarindo, for example, the volcanic features of Rincón de la Vieja and the wetlands of Palo

Ecotourism

Verde are easily reached. Tango Mar is midway between the Cabo Blanco Absolute Nature Reserve and Curu National Wildlife Refuge, while all of these resorts have local trails through the dry tropical forest.

ECOTOURISM

Tourism is one of the fastest growing aspects of the world economy and 'ecotourism' occupies a considerable chunk of this. Kenya pioneered the concept of ecotourism, with Costa Rica following closely behind and providing a model for other Latin American countries. But what exactly does ecotourism mean?

The Ecotourism Society defines the term as:
'Responsible travel to natural areas that conserves the environment and improves the welfare of local people.'
So ecotourism should ideally:
• Minimize the negative environmental aspects of mainstream tourism
• Contribute to conservation efforts, by protecting ecosystems and encouraging biological diversity.

Below: Rainforest lodges have become an important part of the accommodation on offer to the ecotourist, particularly at the lower end of the market.

Introduction

Costa Ricans speak Castilian Spanish, but thankfully it is spoken more slowly. The pronunciation, however, is more akin to that spoken in Andalucía or South America, with none of the soft lisping 'c's or 'z's of Madrid Spanish. It is also more formal, with *usted* (you) being used rather than the informal *tu*, while the prefix *Don* or *Doña* should always be used when speaking to an older person. There is also a tendency to use diminutives. *Tico*, for example, has been adopted by Costa Ricans as a self-deprecating way of referring to themselves. *Pura Vida* (or pure life) is a phrase that one often comes across, particularly in advertising.

• Employ local people to manage natural areas, thereby sharing socio-economic benefits with the indigenous community.

Unfortunately, ecotourism has often become a popular tourism sales pitch, with some companies making completely false claims for their eco-credentials. The best advice is to read between the lines and sort out whether or not their claims are justified and whether the tour provider is adhering to sound environmental principles. Try to find out what percentage of the firm's profits go back into the local community. The same approach should be applied to so-called eco-hotels and eco-lodges. Ask questions such as: Do they use solar power or alternative energy sources? Do they use recycled products? What is their waste treatment policy? Do they reduce temperatures for laundry water and do they encourage changing sheets and towels less frequently?

Ecotourism has a long history in Costa Rica. It has always attracted naturalists and field biologists, largely from North America, with research groups such as the Organization for Tropical Studies using Costa Rica as a base for their work. Although the country's national parks provide the main attraction for eco-visitors, there are a number of private conservation areas, such as the Monteverde development, set up by American Quakers, which has become an immense ecotourism success story. Ecotourism really took off in Costa Rica in the late 1980s and although it has levelled off in recent years, it is estimated that ecotourism pours more than half a million dollars annually into the Costa Rican economy. The country now has a good track record in involving local people in ecotourism, by encouraging indigenous craft work, training guides, setting up locally run lodges and accommodation and persuading farmers to give up slash and burn activities and turn to more sustainable forest management.

Sometimes compromises have been necessary. For example, on the Pacific coast, the taking of sea turtle eggs has been a traditional activity. Now local people have been allowed to take the first tranche of eggs and thereafter provide protection for the eggs and hatchlings and act as tourist guides, bringing additional money into the local community. There are, nevertheless, many threats

Ecotourism

to Costa Rica's ecological success story. One of the greatest is the growth of the agro-export industry, as typified by the production of bananas, which relies on cheap labour and the strong use of pesticides. The hands of bananas grow in blue plastic pesticide-lined bags, which often blow into rivers where they are fatally consumed by wildlife, such as manatees. Pollution from banana and oil palm plantations has also been responsible for killing off many stretches of Costa Rica's coral reefs. There is also a massive problem with waste disposal as the population grows and the consumer society takes hold. Illegal logging threatens many of the country's primary rainforests, while poaching of rare birds and animals still goes on. The problem is that Costa Rica has neither the finance nor the manpower to police these threats.

Responsible Tourism

There is much that the visitor can do to be a responsible tourist and protect the natural environment:

• Choose a tour operator and hotel with a genuine approach to ecotourism and the environment.
• Choose a locally owned hotel rather than one owned by a large foreign chain.
• Use hotel water and electricity sparingly to preserve supplies, which may have been diverted from local areas.
• Read widely beforehand on the types of wildlife you are likely to encounter. The more information you have, the less likely you are to disturb the wildlife.
• Wear clothing colours that blend in with the local landscape, minimizing disturbance to wildlife. When walking, stay on trails to lessen the impact on the forest.
• Avoid buying souvenirs that have been made from local wildlife, such as coral and turtle shells, unless they have been sustainably produced. Instead, buy craft items that have been locally made, thereby helping to maintain indigenous skills.
• Respect cultural differences in language and dress. Always ask permission before taking a person's photograph.
• Above all, of course, leave no litter. To help with this, use recyclable materials, such as glass bottles; avoid using excessive plastic bags and other containers; use rechargeable batteries; use recycled paper whenever possible.

Mutualism and Parasitism

Mutualism is an ecological relationship where both parties benefit. A good example would be of a bee pollinating a plant. In the case of parasitism, one of the species is harmed while the other benefits, as in the case of leeches. Note that epiphytes, which commonly grow on trees in the wetter parts of Costa Rica, are not parasitic – they live ON the tree, but not OFF it, i.e. they do not harm it.

NORTH CARIBBEAN CONSERVATION AREA

The Caribbean coastal lowlands of Costa Rica are part of the coastline that stretches from Guatemala to Panama. They are entirely within Limón Province and have for centuries been the most isolated part of Costa Rica, cut off by the physical barriers of the central cordilleras. Despite the building of the 'jungle railway' at the end of the 19th century, it was not until the Guápiles Highway was completed in the late 1980s that communications with the region improved.

This is the most culturally diverse area of Costa Rica. When Minor Keith built the railway from San José, he brought in black labourers from Jamaica and many of these people stayed on to work in the banana plantations. Today, about one third of the province's population of 250,000 are of Afro-Caribbean origin, with their own culture, Creole cooking, English patois and Protestant religion.

A tourist industry is fast developing in the area, with naturalists and birders particularly attracted to the Tortuguero National Park, while the Barra del Colorado is equally good for wildlife as well as being Costa Rica's best venue for sport fishing.

Tortuguero Top Ten

Sea Turtles
River Turtles
River Otters
Jacunas
Caiman
Sloths
Kingfishers
Basilisk Lizards
Anhingas

Opposite top to bottom:
Tourists leave a lodge for a bird-watching cruise around the creeks of the Tortuguero National Park; Leaf-cutter Ants are busy on the forest floor in the Tortuguero National Park; a Caiman, the smaller cousin of the Crocodile, is common in the Tortuguero Channels.

North Caribbean Conservation Area

Tortuguero National Park

Tortuguero National Park

Location: North Caribbean coast.
Size: 19,000ha (36,100 acres).
Altitude: Just above sea level.
Of Interest: Lowland rainforest, threatened by logging and farming in the west of the region.

Tortuguero National Park

The word *tortuguero* translates as 'turtle catcher' and the park has some 22 miles (35km) of somewhat desolate beach on which four species of sea turtles nest. The beach is not suitable for swimming, due to the rip tides, sharks and barracudas, but there are usually sea birds around, such as Royal Terns, Frigate Birds and Brown Pelicans, while waders such as plovers and sandpipers can be seen along the shoreline. On this sand ridge, some 200–300m (650–985ft) wide, is the small village of Tortuguero, a soporific settlement of around 600 people, with palm groves, well-mown lawns and a profusion of tropical shrubs. Sandy paths run around the village with its wooden houses with tin roofs, an attractive little church and the occasional store and bar. There is a small information kiosk in the centre of the village and close by is a new visitors' centre, which shows a brief video on turtle conservation. There is a short but well-maintained nature trail nearby. A donation on entry to the centre is much appreciated.

Behind the sand ridge is the main waterway of the park, running parallel with the coastline. Unfortunately the earthquakes in the 1990s raised the level of the land, so that only boats with a shallow draft can use the waterway today, but the depth is sufficient to bring tourists in *lanchas* to the lodges around

Right: Dense rainforest, rich in birds, butterflies and other wildlife, lines the banks of the Tortuguero Channels.

Tortuguero National Park

Tortuguero village. To the west of the main waterway is a maze of channels penetrating into the rainforest, which is full of wildlife such as birds, reptiles, amphibians, butterflies and mammals. Some 400 species of birds have been recorded, along with 57 types of amphibians, 111 forms of reptiles and 60 mammals species, including many of the country's endangered animals, such as jaguars, tapirs, ocelots, cougars and river otters. The wide channels make bird-watching easy and the visitor would be unlucky not to see a variety of toucans, kingfishers, anhingas, parrots and jacunas. The waterways and canals support 50 types of fish, plus caimans, crocodiles, river otters and seven types of freshwater turtle. Manatees can occasionally be seen under the water, but these fascinating mammals have retreated to the calmer waters of the western creeks. The exotic shrubs in the grounds of the lodges attract swarms of butterflies, while the forest trees provide a home for mammals including three types of monkey, anteaters, sloths and numerous species of bat, one of which catches fish by sonar. Canoes can be hired to explore the rivers and creeks, with early morning being the best time for the maximum number of sightings. The forest trails give opportunities for observing ants, including Bullet Ants, whose bites can cause 24 hours of excruciating pain, and Army Ants who form a swarm of often over a million to attack their prey. The most noticeable, however, are the Leaf-cutter Ants, often seen in long lines crossing forest trails and carrying leaf pieces to their underground colony. The leaves decay to form a mulch which develops a fungus. The fungus is then fed to the ant colony. The humid atmosphere, however, attracts less welcome insect wildlife and the visitor should come well protected with some form of insect repellent.

Turtle Protection

During the 1950s the turtle population of Tortuguero came to the attention of an American biologist, Dr Archie Carr, of Florida University. Concerned for the future of the turtles, he set up, in 1959, the Caribbean Conservation Corporation to study and protect sea turtles within the region. A tagging programme was organized and it continues to this day. Carr worked with the Costa Rican government to establish Tortuguero as a sanctuary where the endangered turtles could nest unmolested. The sanctuary was set up in 1963 and the area became a national park in 1970.

Sea Turtles

The Caribbean coast of Costa Rica is the principal nesting site for the Atlantic Green Sea Turtle, some 30,000 of which come ashore to lay their eggs from July until October, with the greatest numbers arriving in September. The Green Turtles can weigh as much as 100 tons, but these are eclipsed by the giant Leatherback Turtle, whose shell or carapace can grow to 5m (16ft), making it the largest reptile in the world. The Leatherback nests to the south of Tortuguero village from February to April. Hawksbill and Loggerhead Turtles also lay their eggs here. Egg laying is at night and the mass arrivals of the turtles are known as *arribadas*. There are strict rules for visitors – no one is allowed on the beach at night unless accompanied by a guide, no cameras or flashlights are permitted and only 200 people can view in any one hour. Nevertheless, to watch these huge sea creatures come ashore to lay their eggs is a supreme wildlife experience, rivalled only by the spectacular scene some weeks later of the hatchlings scampering their way to the sea, running the gauntlet of predators. Despite legislation and official protection, poachers still steal eggs from the beaches for their supposed aphrodisiac qualities and catch turtles at sea for their meat and turtle soup.

Toucans

There are six species of toucan in Costa Rica and they are identified by their disproportionately large bills which, despite their size, are surprisingly light. Birds of the forest canopy, they are frequently seen in the Tortuguero area, where they feed on fruit, seeds, insects, lizards and small snakes. Toucans nest in holes in trees, where they lay two to four white eggs. Their calls are raucously unmusical. The two largest species are the Chestnut-mandibled Toucan (*Ramphastos swainsonii*) and the Keel-billed Toucan (*Ramphastos sufuratus*). The smaller toucans include two species of aricari and two species of toucanet.

Below: A Green Turtle hatchling emerges from the sand on Tortuguero beach. At this stage of their life they are easy prey to predators and only a small proportion survive to adulthood.

Basilisk Lizards

The Tortuguero National Park is as good a place as any in Costa Rica to encounter the basilisk or 'Jesus Christ' lizard. The basilisk (*Basiliscus basiliscus*) is common along many lowland watercourses and they gain their nickname

Tortuguero National Park

from their ability to 'walk on water', running over the surface of rivers and streams when they are disturbed. They actually skip along on their rear legs, often for many metres, in an upright position. Juvenile basilisks are better at walking on water than the adults, who, when they become too heavy, have to resort to swimming. Basilisks are semi-arboreal and will spend much of their time climbing in the low branches of trees above the water. Basilisks are generally brown in colour with noticeable head crests. They will grow up to a metre in length, but much of this is taken up with the tail. The females lay a clutch of up to 18 eggs several times a year. The hatchling lizards are unprotected by the adults and are very vulnerable to predation – probably less than 10% survive to adulthood.

Getting There

Access to Tortuguero is by boat or plane only. Boats can be boarded at Puerto Hamburgo just to the north of Moín or alternatively visitors can come down the Sarapiquí River from Puerto Viejo. Tortuguero has its own small airstrip, with daily flights to and from San José run by SANSA or Travelair.

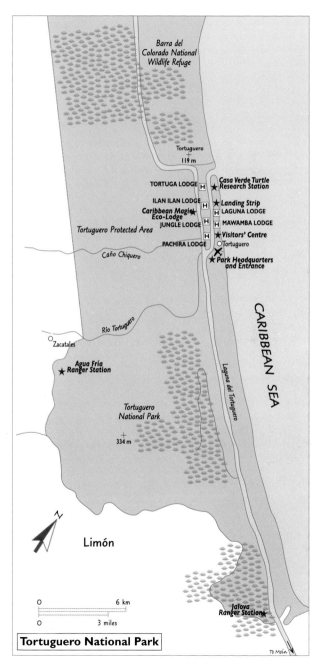

Barra del Colorado National Wildlife Refuge

Tortuguero
119 m

TORTUGA LODGE H — Casa Verde Turtle Research Station

ILAN ILAN LODGE H — Landing Strip
Caribbean Magic Eco-Lodge — H LAGUNA LODGE
Tortuguero Protected Area — JUNGLE LODGE H — H MAWAMBA LODGE
H — Visitors' Centre
PACHIRA LODGE — O Tortuguero
Park Headquarters and Entrance

Caño Chiquero

CARIBBEAN SEA

Zacatales
Río Tortuguero

Agua Fría Ranger Station

Laguna del Tortuguero

Tortuguero National Park
334 m

Limón

0 — 6 km
0 — 3 miles

Jalova Ranger Station

Tortuguero National Park

To Moín

North Caribbean Conservation Area

Accommodation

Accommodation is limited to simple, clean *cabinas* in Tortuguero village and around 10 'jungle lodges', which are heavily used by two- and three-day package tours from San José. The two lodges on the village side of the canal have the advantage of the facilities of the village and the proximity of the turtle nesting beach. The other lodges need to transport their visitors by boat. Most tours include guided forest walks, boat trips and turtle-watching if it is the season for it. Some tours provide a walk to the top of Cerro Tortuguero, an old volcanic plug in the north of the area, which rises to 119m (300ft) and gives superb views over the surrounding forest, waterways and coast.

Pachira Lodge: This luxury Costa Rican-owned lodge has comfortable cabins, a good restaurant and a sizeable pool. Tel: 2256 7080, www.pachiralodge.com

Tortuga Lodge: Owned by Costa Rica Expeditions. Comfortable, with good facilities. Tel: 2257 0766, www.costaricaexpeditions.com

Ilan Ilan Lodge: Owned by Mitur Tours. One of the more basic lodges. Tel: 2255 2262.

Barra del Colorado National Wildlife Refuge

CARIBBEAN SEA

NICARAGUA

Isla Calero · Barra del Colorado · ★ Sport Fishing

San Juan · Isla Brava

Barra del Colorado National Wildlife Refuge

Heredia

Limón

Suerte

○ Canta Gallo

Casa Verde Turtle Research Station

Tortuguero

Tortuguero Protected Area

Barra del Colorado National Wildlife Refuge

The Barra del Colorado National Wildlife Refuge is situated between Tortuguero and the Nicaraguan border. Although ecologically similar to Tortuguero, much of it has been cleared for agriculture as its protected status came rather later. Indeed, a boat trip along the San Juan River,

Barra del Colorado National Wildlife Refuge

which forms the border with Nicaragua, shows considerable contrast between the two countries, with thick forest to the north and much farmland on the Costa Rican side. Nevertheless, there is plenty of rainforest producing species similar in range to those at Tortuguero. The reserve is largely comprised of the delta of the Río San Juan which drains Lake Nicaragua. The Río Colorado is the main distributary on the Costa Rican side and it is at the mouth of this river that one finds the village of Barra del Colorado, divided into Barra Norte on the river's north side and Barra Sur to the south. The airstrip is at Barra Sur.

The 2000 or so inhabitants of the river delta are a mixture of Afro-Caribbean, *indigenas*, Costa Ricans and some Nicaraguans who fled across the border during that country's Civil War. Barra's proximity to the instability in Nicaragua has held up tourist development, but this is likely to change in the not too distant future.

With an average temperature of 26°C (79°F) and an annual rainfall of 4000mm (160in), Barra has a similar climate and natural vegetation to Tortuguero. The wildlife is equally good, particularly as there is less disturbance, but the reserve is less accessible and there are few trails, so that most viewing is by boat. You are certain to see mammals such as Spider Monkeys, Howler Monkeys and Three-toed Sloths, while reptiles include crocodiles, caiman and the ubiquitous iguana. There is a wide range of forest and water birds, such as toucans, jacanas, Green Macaws, parrots, trogons and a whole selection of the heron family. This is also the best location in Costa Rica to see the endangered Manatee go gliding past under the water.

Many people, however, come to Barra del Colorado for the sport fishing. The best season for tarpon is from February to late May, while snook are caught in droves during September and October, though there is good fishing to be had at any time of the year. Other fish available include barracuda and rainbow bass, while there is deep-sea fishing offshore for both marlin and sailfish. Most lodges operate a 'catch and release' policy. Tours can be arranged in San José and usually consist of three- or five-night packages. A few of the lodges also provide packages for naturalists.

Barra del Colorado National Wildlife Refuge

Location: Between Tortuguero National Park and the Nicaraguan border on the Caribbean coast.

Size: 92,000ha (227,000 acres).

Altitude: Sea level.

Of Interest: Full range of forest and water wildlife, plus sport fishing.

Accommodation: Confined to fishing lodges. Silver King Lodge, tel: 2381 1403, is the most de luxe lodge, with no expense spared.

Barra del Colorado Top Ten

Manatees
Spider and Howler Monkeys
Sloths
Anhinga
Green Macaws
Trogons
Blue Morpho butterfly
River Otters
Kingfishers
Glossy Ibis

North Caribbean Conservation Area

Creole Cooking

Visitors bored with the bland beans-and-rice cooking of much of Costa Rica (and the international food found in many of the hotels) will enjoy the more spicy offerings of the Creole cuisine of the Caribbean lowlands. Creole cooking is typified by the use of coconut milk and spices such as cumin, coriander, peppers, chillies and cloves. Vegetables include ackee, the potato-like yam and breadfruit. Plantains are widely used and often fried as fritters. Sweet desserts and herbal teas complete the tasty Creole menu.

Shark Territory

For much of the north Caribbean shore, swimming, surfing and snorkelling are not options. Rip tides, heavy waves and pollution from banana boats are just some of the hazards. The main danger, however, is the presence of sharks. Many of them come into quite shallow water and are serious predators of baby turtles as they scuttle into the sea.

A dangerous species is the Bull Shark (*Carcharhinus leucas*), which is aggressive and unpredictable. The diet of Bull Sharks includes fish, dolphins, birds and even terrestrial mammals. Bull Sharks are thought to be responsible for the majority of shark attacks on humans. They can often be seen in the Barra area, migrating up the Río San Juan to breed in the freshwater Lake Nicaragua. Species that are able to move from salt to fresh water without apparent ill effect are described as euryhaline. Until quite recently, it was thought that the sharks in Lake Nicaragua were a separate species because there was no way that the sharks could move in or out of the lake, but it was then discovered that they were able to jump rapids in the same way as salmon. Subsequently, Bull Sharks tagged in the lake were later recovered from the Caribbean.

Bull Sharks breed in the summer. After gestating for about a year, a Bull Shark may give birth to as many as 13 live young, which are about 70cm (28in) at birth and take 10 years to reach maturity.

Anhingas

There are four species of the widely distributed anhinga, one of which (*Anhinga anhinga*) is found in the lakes, lagoons and marshes of Costa Rica. They are distinguished from the closely related cormorants by their long pointed bills and longer kinked necks. They are largely black in colour (although the females have buff necks), with silvery spots and streaks on the mantle and wing coverts.

The anhingas' preferred habitat requires trees where they can perch and spread their wings out to dry after fishing. This may also help digestion. (Another less serious explanation is that the outspread wings are indicating the size of the 'one that got

Barra del Colorado National Wildlife Refuge

away'!) When swimming on the surface of the water the body is almost invisible, giving rise to the name 'snakebird'. The anhinga swims stealthily underwater, catching fish with a swift stab of the bill – they are also known as darters and the Costa Rican name is Pato Aguja or needle duck. They will also eat small turtles, young caiman, frogs and snakes.

Above: Anhinga (or Snakebird) in flight, distinguished by the silvery spots on the wing coverts. It often swims with only the snake-like head and neck visible.

Anhingas build their nests in trees, either in small groups or in larger colonies with other water birds. They breed after approximately three years and usually mate for life. Both the adult birds regurgitate food to the young, who fledge after about five weeks. The anhinga is locally common in Costa Rica and is not considered threatened.

SOUTH CARIBBEAN CONSERVATION AREA

The south Caribbean coast is dominated by the provincial capital and small port of Puerto Limón which, with its suburbs, contains around 70,000 people. It is a busy port, but has lost much of its trade recently to Moín, where the larger banana boats make use of the deeper water. Cruise liners, however, now make frequent calls. Offshore is the small rocky island of La Uvita, where Columbus made his first landfall on what is now Costa Rica. Because of earthquake destruction, Limón today has none of the rather dilapidated architectural charm of some other Central American ports. In the centre of Limón is the attractive Vargas Park, with a bandstand, some faded murals and a stand of royal palms complete with resident sloths. Apart from the Town Hall, with some interesting iron grillwork, there is little else to see.

Things improve to the south of Puerto Limón, where Highway 36 runs to the Panama border at Sixaola, passing through Cahuita (where a marine national park protects the coral reef), Puerto Viejo (one of the best surfing spots in Costa Rica), some *indigenas* reserves and the little visited, but beautiful Gandoca-Manzanillo National Wildlife Refuge.

Cahuita Top Ten

Coral reef
Tropical reef fish
Sloths
Beach and land crabs
Coatis
Raccoons
Agoutis
Armadillos
White-faced Monkeys
Howler Monkeys

Opposite top to bottom:
The Nine-banded Armadillo is found in the forested areas of the Caribbean and Pacific coasts; Puerto Viejo is a popular surfing spot and attracts backpackers in good numbers; a banana plantation in Limon province – bananas are a major export to many parts of the world.

South Caribbean Conservation Area

Opposite: The Cahuita
National Park consists of an
offshore coral reef and a beach
backed by rainforest and
mangroves.

Cahuita National Park

Located on a point some 42km (26 miles) south of Puerto Limón
is the small village of Cahuita. Its sand and gravel streets support a
population of mainly English-speaking blacks, descendants of the
Afro-Caribbean fishermen who settled here in the mid-1900s.
Tourism has developed considerably and the town has become
popular with young backpackers. New hotels and restaurants are
gradually spreading along the Playa Negra, a black sand beach to
the north of the village, while south of the village is a beach of
white sand backed by rainforest. Between the two is a headland,
with a coral reef offshore, making up the Cahuita National Park.
Covering a mere 1067ha (2636 acres), the park nevertheless
contains a wide variety of species, both on the land and in the sea.
The coral reef is just offshore and it is possible to wade out to it,
although local boatmen can take you out. Snorkelling is excellent,
particularly during the drier parts of the year (Feb–Apr and
Sep–Oct). At other times heavy rain falling in the Talamanca
Mountains swells the local rivers with silt, making water visibility
poor. Although the reef is less attractive since the 1991
earthquake, you should see massive brain corals, elkhorn, blue
staghorn, sea fans, tubipora and frondlike gorgonians. In addition,
more than 500 species of fish have been identified around the
reef, including angelfish, rock beauty and blue parrotfish. Fish also
congregate around two old shipwrecks, whose cannons can easily
be seen. Swimmers and snorkellers should be aware of the local
black sea urchins, which have large and vicious black spines.

Although Cahuita is basically a marine park, just under half
comprises beach and a coastal strip of rainforest and mangroves.
The beach is inhabited by red landcrabs and bright blue fiddler
crabs with their huge claws. A trail runs in and out of the forest
behind the beach, joining the two ranger stations. Animal life
abounds, with the possibility of seeing Coatis, Raccoons, Sloths,
Agoutis, Armadillos and both Howler and White-faced Monkeys.
The bird-watching is excellent, with Green Ibis, Rufous Kingfisher,
toucans and parrots amongst many others. The small rivers
running into the reserve are home to a variety of herons. The
vegetation is also interesting and includes the Breadfruit tree
(*Artocarpus altilis*), believed to have been introduced to the area
by Captain Bligh in 1793. It can reach 20m (60ft) in height and its

Cahuita National Park

Location: South Caribbean coast.
Size: 1067ha (2636 acres).
Altitude: Sea level.
Climate: warm and humid, with
the chance of rain on any day
of the year.
Of Interest: Coral reef, tropical
rainforest and mangroves.

Cahuita National Park

Despite Costa Rica's lengthy tropical coastline, there are only two areas of coral reef, both in the south Caribbean area – at Cahuita and at the Gandoca-Manzanillo National Wildlife Refuge. Coral reefs are made up of the secretions of small animals called polyps, filter feeders that build a protective limestone layer around themselves. Over 35 types of coral have been identified at Cahuita, but nevertheless the future is not good. Corals require warm, clean salt water in order to survive. A tragedy occurred in 1992 when an earthquake raised the sea bed about three metres, exposing the coral at low tide, thereby killing off the upper part of the reef. Other threats have been man-made. The growth of oil palm and banana plantations has meant that large amounts of chemicals have been washed into the sea, affecting the purity of the water and causing plankton blooms that cut out the sunlight. In addition, logging activity denudes the slopes, causing large amounts of silt to be washed into the sea, which again can block out the sunlight.

glossy green leaves are often over a metre in length. The tree gets its name from its fruit, which can be cooked to give a bread-like substance that is rich in carbohydrate. All parts of the tree yield latex, which is used for boat caulking. Another tree found in the area is the *cawi* or *sangregao*. The Miskito word gave its name to Cahuita, which translates as 'the headland of cawi trees'.

A few kilometres north of Cahuita is the estuary of the Río Estrella, where a small wildlife sanctuary, Aviarios del Caribe, is based on an island in the estuary. There are numerous birds and animals at the sanctuary and popular guided kayak tours of the estuary will turn up a wide range of wildlife, including River Otters, Caimans and many types of heron.

Just 13km (8 miles) south of Cahuita is the laid-back village of Puerto Viejo de Talamanca, which has become very popular in recent years with a surfing and backpacking crowd. The main attraction without doubt is the surf, which is the best on the Caribbean coast. The famous 'salsa brava' wave is at its best between December and March. A local organization called ATEC (Asociacion Talamanqueña de Ecoturismo y Conservación), which

South Caribbean Conservation Area

Indigenas Reserves

The *indigenas* people of Costa Rica form a mere 1% of the population and most of these are fully integrated into society. The government, however, has decided that their culture should be preserved and in 1972 it set up 22 *indigenas* reserves, mainly in remote areas, such as Talamanca, so that *indigenas* people can live in self-governing communities. The reserves have very little in the way of infrastructure and in most cases have not become tourist attractions. However, to the southwest of Cahuita are three reserves — KekoLdi, Talamanca-Bribrí and Cabecar — on the northern slopes of the Talamanca mountains. The reserves have been incorporated into La Amistad International Park and permits are needed for entry. These can be arranged through ATEC, who run trips to the KekoLdi reserve. The *indigenas* make a living by raising iguanas, making and selling baskets and being involved in reforestation and other conservation projects.

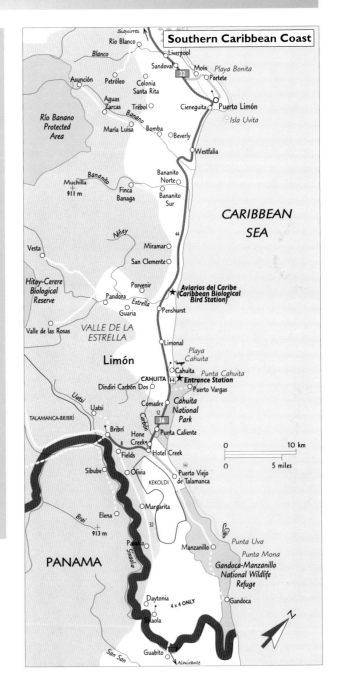

Gandoca-Manzanillo National Wildlife Refuge

is devoted to ecologically sustainable development, runs tours, including guided walks through the rainforest, snorkelling trips to the reef and fishing trips in dugout canoes. The road south from Puerto Viejo has recently been paved, making it easier to reach the villages of Punta Uva and Manzanillo, with superb beaches backed by coconut palms.

Getting There
Take the Guápiles Highway from San José, then proceed south on Highway 36 from Puerto Limón.

Accommodation
In this area you will find mainly the mid- to low-range option. There is plenty of choice for backpackers.

Hotel Suerre: Eastern end of Puerto Limón, tel: 2710 7551. Country club hotel with pool and tennis courts.

Hotel Cahuita: Next to the national park, tel: 2755 0233. Motel-style cabins with pool.

Gandoca-Manzanillo National Wildlife Refuge
This recent addition to the Costa Rican national wildlife refuge system stretches from the village of Manzanillo to the Sixaola River, which forms the border with Panama. It consists of 65% rainforest habitat, with the remainder being marine habitat. The offshore coral reef is in better shape than the one at Cahuita, although the corals have not yet developed formations so large. There are eleven species of sponges recorded, which are endemic to the area. Naturally, there are excellent snorkelling possibilities. The terrestrial part of the reserve includes a number of habitats, such as a beach boasting four types of nesting sea turtle (Leatherback, Loggerhead, Green and Hawksbill), the peaceful Gandoca estuary backed by red mangroves with the country's only population of oysters, and 400ha (752 acres) of swamp forest in which the most common tree is the raphia palm, which claims to be the plant with the largest leaves in the world – its fronds can reach 12m (39ft) or more. The rainforest section has recorded over 350 species of birds, while the estuary is a good

Gandoca-Manzanillo National Wildlife Refuge

Location: Between the village of Manzanillo and the Panama border on the Caribbean coast.
Size: 5013ha (12,387 acres) marine, 4436ha (10,961 acres) terrestrial, 9449ha (23,348 acres) in all.
Altitude: Sea level.
Of Interest: Coral reef and tropical fish, nesting beach turtles, rainforest birds and animals.
Getting There: Guápiles Highway from San José to Puerto Limón. Local bus to Manzanillo.
Accommodation: Little of quality in the immediate area, but plenty of cabinas and bungalows.

South Caribbean Conservation Area

spot to see the endangered manatee. Over 500 species of marine and freshwater fish have been recorded, while there are three resident species of dolphin – the bottlenose, the Atlantic spotted and the extremely rare tucuxi. Clearly, Gandoca-Manzanillo is an absolute gem and well worth the effort of getting there.

Manatees
(Trichechus Manatus)

These aquatic marine mammals are sometimes known as 'sea cows' and can be found in estuarine locations all along

Above: Mother and baby Manatee. These slow moving mammals can be seen along the Caribbean coast, but are becoming increasingly threatened, largely due to the activities of man.

Costa Rica's Caribbean coast. To actually spot a Manatee, however, is extremely difficult. They are highly susceptible to disturbance from boats and have learnt to move to quieter creeks. They are thought to have evolved from four-legged animals some 60 million years ago and are closely related to the elephant. They are mainly herbivores, spending most of their time grazing in shallow waters at depths of 1–2m (3.3–6.5ft). They can grow to lengths of 2.7–3m (9–10ft) and can weigh over 500kg (1200lb). Most Manatees swim at around 3–5 miles per hour, which makes it difficult for them to avoid motorboats, so that many have been seen with slashes caused by propellers. Nevertheless, Manatees have been recorded as living for over 60 years. They were once hunted for their meat along the Caribbean coast, although this rarely happens today, with sharks and crocodiles being their main natural predators. However, man is still the main danger to the Manatee, largely due to watercraft strikes.

Hitoy-Cerere Biological Reserve

Approximately 60km (37 miles) south of Limón in the Valle de la Estrella is the Hitoy-Cerere Biological Reserve, one of the least visited parks in Costa Rica, largely due to its extreme

Hitoy-Cerere Biological Reserve

inaccessibility. Its rugged terrain and high rainfall – an astounding 4000mm (158in) a year with no dry season – will deter all but the most enthusiastic naturalist. The name refers to the two rivers and comes from the Bribri language, *hitoy* meaning 'moss-covered' and *cerere* referring to 'clear waters'. The habitat is dense tropical rainforest, with tall trees, dripping with epiphytes, bromeliads, orchids and lianas.

This is one of the best areas of the country to see large cats, while there are good numbers of peccaries, margays, tapirs, agoutis and monkeys, such as White-faced and Howlers. The approach road to the reserve reveals trees full of the colonial nests of Montezuma and Chestnut-headed Oropendolas, while in the forest you could see toucans, parrots and the rare Squirrel Cuckoo. This is also one of the last strongholds of the extremely endangered Harpy Eagle. There are few facilities at the reserve, but there are a few trails; these, however, are very challenging and only for the experienced tropical hiker.

Armadillos

There are about 20 species of armadillo with a range from Central USA to the southern tip of South America. Of these, two occur in Costa Rica: the Naked-tailed Armadillo, which is totally nocturnal and rarely seen, and the Nine-banded Armadillo (*Dasypus novemcinctus*), which is a common resident of forests and thickets throughout the country. The armadillo has a brownish, hairless body with around nine movable bone plates around its middle. It has a long snout and an even longer ringed tail. When threatened, it curls up in a ball, and with its soft abdomen protected, there is little that an attacker can do. Armadillos are slow-moving, however, and are frequently run over by vehicles. They are omnivorous, feeding on a variety of insects and small invertebrates, when their long claws come in useful. The claws are also used for digging out burrows used for sleeping and breeding. The armadillo's breeding habits are unusual in that the female produces four young at a time, all from a single fertilized egg, so that the babies are effectively identical quadruplets. Nine-banded armadillos are thought to be common and not endangered, but owing to their partially nocturnal lifestyles, this is largely guesswork.

Hitoy-Cerere Biological Reserve

Location: 60km (37miles) south of Puerto Limón in the Valle de la Estrella; 227km (141 miles) from San José.

Size: 9154ha (22,620 acres).

Altitude: 150m (430ft) rising to 1000m (3280ft).

Climate: Hot and wet throughout the year with 4000mm (158in) of rainfall. The average temperature is 29°C (84°F).

Of Interest: One of the best reserves in the country for wild cats; two species of monkey. Birds include both Oropendolas, toucans and parrots.

THE NORTHERN CONSERVATION ZONE

The Northern Zone of Costa Rica stretches from the Cordillera Central to the border with Nicaragua. The mountain area is dominated by the active cone of Volcán Arenal, rising to 1633m (5358ft). Further north, stretching towards the border and to the west, are tropical plains known as *llaneras*. The northern boundary with Nicaragua is marked by the Río San Juan, the border officially on the Costa Rican bank.

The vegetation of the area is mainly scattered forest and grassland, with trees packed more densely in the east. Much of the woodland, however, has been cleared for cattle *fincas*, banana plantations, rice and fruit growing. The mountains to the west of the region, particularly around Monteverde, are covered in cloud forest.

The infrastructure is quite good in the south of the region, with a comprehensive road network and regular flights from San José. On the *llaneras*, however, communications are poor. Small market towns such as Puerto Viejo de Sarapiquí and San Carlos have grown markedly in recent years, but the most startling growth has occurred at Fortuna, which has become a major tourist centre, specializing in adventure activities such as kayaking, whitewater rafting, horse riding and windsurfing on Lake Arenal.

Caño Negro Top Ten

Garfish
Tarpon
Roseate Spoonbill
Wood Stork
Sloths
Osprey
Caiman
Crocodiles
Nicaraguan Grackle
Jabiru Storks

Opposite top to bottom: View of Volcán Arenal erupting from the Balneario Tabacón; an unusual picture of a Black Vulture and a Turkey Vulture sitting on the same branch; the Skywalk at Monteverde – a series of trails and suspension bridges through the cloud forest canopy.

The Northern Conservation Zone

Climate

The climate is generally hot and wet, but there is a distinct dry season from Jan–Mar, especially in the northwest. The *llaneras* are flooded in the wet season, resulting in a good habitat for migrating wildfowl.

Near to Puerto Viejo are two biological research stations, both of which welcome visitors: La Selva (see panel, page 53), and Rara Avis (see panel, page 54).

Arenal Volcano National Park

Arenal is the most spectacularly active volcano in Costa Rica, if not the world. After being dormant for centuries an earthquake blew the top off in 1968, sending ash, volcanic bombs and lava over a wide area. The villages of Tabacón and Pueblo Nuevo were totally destroyed, killing all the inhabitants along with thousands of

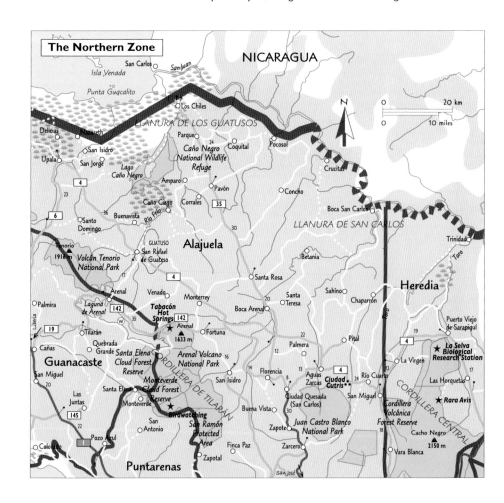

Arenal Volcano National Park

cattle. Since then, Arenal has been continuously active on a daily basis, with large eruptions in 1973, 1975, 1993, 2000, 2003 and 2005. Rising to 1633m (5358ft), Arenal is everyone's idea of what a volcano should look like, with its perfect cone shape and frequent spectacular activity, making it one of the country's foremost tourist attractions. Needless to say, it is extremely dangerous and foolhardy to walk anywhere near the summit, with its crater some 150m (492ft) deep and the eruptive activity highly unpredictable. It is possible to hike around the base, but most tours view the volcano from the west side, where there are fresh lava flows. The summit is often covered in cloud during the day, particularly during the wet season, but night viewing can be spectacular, with glowing lava flows and red hot rocks being thrown from the crater and rolling down the sides. Most of the streams flowing off the flanks of Volcán Arenal have been naturally heated and are often full of beneficial minerals. At Balneario Tabacón, a valley has been converted into a complex of eight pools of various temperatures ranging from 27°C (80°F) to 39°C (102°F). The area around the volcano was designated a national park in 1991. For obvious reasons, there is little in the way of wildlife in the immediate vicinity of the volcano, but there is plenty to be seen in the forested fringes of the park. A particularly recommended tour is to the Arenal Hanging Bridges, a 3km (2-mile) hike through the rainforest involving crossing 15 precarious and narrow suspension bridges varying in length from 5–100m (16–330ft), often at canopy height. A good range of wildlife is guaranteed, with birds such as Blue Gray Tanager, Summer Tanager, Buff-throated Saltador, various woodpeckers, Rufous-tailed Jacamar, Rufous Motmot and many others. Coatimundis and Howler Monkeys are also common. Night walks are a speciality here – remember that 80% of Costa Rica's mammals are nocturnal.

La Selva Biological Research Station

Just 4km (2.5 miles) to the south of Puerto Viejo, La Selva is owned by the Organization of Tropical Studies and concentrates on investigation into the biological aspects of rainforests and other tropical habitats. Although research is the main focus of the station, visitors are welcome (do book ahead) and there are some 25 rather muddy trails through the primary and secondary forest, abandoned farmland and pasture. Not surprisingly, over 400 species of birds have been recorded here, including parrots, toucans, hummingbirds and trogons, while mammals include coatis, agoutis, peccaries and three species of monkeys. Less welcome are the 56 species of snake found on the reserve, seven of which are venomous. An amazing 450 tree species have been identified. Little wonder that scientists from all over the world have studied at La Selva.

Vultures

Look up into the skies anywhere in Costa Rica, particularly in the dry season, and any black speck to be seen floating around in the thermals is likely to be a vulture. These birds, which look so ugly on the ground with their bare heads and somewhat revolting scavenging habits, are masters in the sky, soaring and floating majestically. Vultures lack a syrinx and are therefore voiceless except for hisses and low grunts. They are most easily identified by their underwing

The Northern Conservation Zone

Rara Avis

Situated 18km (11 miles) from Puerto Viejo, Rara Avis is a private rainforest reserve, founded by Amos Bien, a North American biologist who came to Costa Rica as a student and never went home. The reserve covers some 1330ha (3280 acres) of pristine forest and is reached directly from Highway 4 at Las Horquetas, from where there is a bone-jarring two-hour tractor journey to the lodge. Rara Avis shows that the rainforest can be both profitable and sustainable without being destroyed. A variety of forest specimens have been developed as ornamental houseplants, raw material is used for wickerwork, exportable orchids have been produced and small family-run butterfly farms have been set up. The inaccessibility of the Rara Avis has meant that there is a lot of wildlife to be seen. Amongst the 500 types of tree, over 300 bird species have been recorded, including rarities such as Great Green Macaws, Blue and Gold Tanagers and Umbrellabirds. Amongst the mammals the jaguar is occasionally seen along with three species of monkey, anteaters, coatis and tapirs. There is a vast range of butterflies and snakes including the deadly Fer-de-lance and Bushmaster. Rara Avis is the place where canopy platforms and walkways were first developed and where Donald Perry invented a prototype aerial tram.

pattern. The most widespread type is the Black Vulture (*Coragyps atratus*), which has light grey tips to its wings. The Black Vulture is catholic in its feeding habits, and as well as carrion it will eat fruit, while it is also a predator of baby sea turtles. The Turkey Vulture (*Cathartes aura*) is also common and has a broad light grey area along the length of the rear part of the underwings. It is seen over both open country and forests, usually alone or in groups of two or three. The King Vulture (*Sarcoramphus papa*) is the largest vulture seen in Costa Rica and other vultures will give way to it at a carcass. It is white in colour, but has black on the rear part of its wings. It prefers at least partly forested areas and is usually solitary. The Lesser Yellow-headed Vulture (*Cathartes burrovianus*) is rare and largely confined to wetland areas in the north, where it will eat the bodies of reptiles and fishes. The smallest of the country's vultures, it is similar to the Turkey Vulture, apart from its distinctly coloured head. All four species are resident in Costa Rica, but many migrate in large numbers flying south in the winter and returning north during the summer.

Caño Negro National Wildlife Refuge

Caño Negro is one of Costa Rica's more remote nature reserves, located on the *llaneras* close to the Nicaraguan border. It is an absolute gem and well worth the detailed planning needed to get there. Most visitors to Caño Negro come from hotels in the San Carlos or Fortuna region and drive to the small town of Los Chiles, and from here transport is by boat to Lago Caño Negro. In the dry season it is possible to take a 4WD vehicle from Upala straight to the hamlet of Caño Negro and the entrance to the refuge.

The habitat at Caño Negro undergoes a remarkable seasonal change. During the wet season, the waters of the Río Frío and other streams that flow off Volcán Tenorio flood the area, creating Lago Caño Negro, a shallow lake of around 800ha (1980 acres), coinciding with the passage of vast numbers of migratory wildfowl. In late February, the dry season begins to set in and the lake gradually dries out, leaving isolated small lagoons and pools along with main channel of the Río Frío. Caño Negro is a paradise for birders, many of whom claim to have seen more species here than at Tortuguero. The most spectacular birds are also the

Caño Negro National Wildlife Refuge

largest, such as Jabiru Storks, and also Wood Storks, Egrets, White Ibis, Glossy Ibis, Black-necked Stilt, Anhingas, Roseate Spoonbills and Ospreys. Wildfowl include Black-bellied Whistling Duck, American Widgeon, Shoveller and Blue-winged Teal. This is also the best place in the country to see the Nicaraguan Grackle. Riverside trees have Howler Monkeys and well-camouflaged sloths, while reptiles such as crocodiles, river turtles and caiman are easily seen by the pools during the dry season. Caño Negro has recently been discovered by anglers and the waters are alive with Tarpon, Snook, Guapote, Bull Shark, and the strange Garfish – half fish and half mammal, with lungs, gills and a nose.

Tarpon

The Atlantic Tarpon (*Megalops atlanticus*) is a popular sport fish. Nicknamed the 'Silver King' due to its size and silvery appearance, it prefers coastal waters and is commonly found in lagoons and estuaries, while it will also travel up rivers. Spawning, however, always takes place at sea. In Costa Rica, it can be seen at Caño Negro refuge and also at Barra Colorado. The top of the Tarpon's body is a greenish blue, while the flanks are silvery. It has a large, upturned mouth and it has the ability when swimming in poorly oxygenated waters to breathe air from the surface. Tarpon have been recorded as reaching 250cm (98in) in length and weighing up to 160kg (350lb). The genus name derives from the Greek adjective *megalo* (meaning 'large') and the noun *opsi* (meaning 'face'). Observers at Caño Negro have reported seeing Tarpon jumping three to five times out of the water, sometimes to a height of twelve feet and doing a somersault in the process – a spectacular sight even if you are not an angler!

The Monteverde Area
Introduction
A visit to the cloud forest area around Monteverde should be on every ecotourist's itinerary. What you will get is an isolated rural community that has protected a vast area of dense cloud forest with a staggering amount of flora and fauna, justly warranting its description as one of the best sanctuaries in the New World tropics. Located approximately 30km (20 miles) southwest of Fortuna, Monteverde is in the higher reaches of the Cordillera de Tilarán, straddling the continental divide at 1440m (4662ft). There

Caño Negro National Wildlife Refuge

Location: On the plains just south of the Nicaraguan border. The nearest town is Los Chiles.

Size: 10,000ha (24,700 acres). The seasonal Lake Caño Negro covers around 800ha (1977 acres).

Altitude: 30–100m (100–330ft).

Habitats: Tropical lowland rainforest, pasture, freshwater marsh, river and lake (think Florida Everglades).

Of Interest: Vast numbers of migratory wildfowl during the wet season. Water birds and reptiles at all times of the year.

Accommodation: There is little near to the reserve. Most visitors stay in the vicinity of Fortuna or San Carlos. Camping is allowed, but there are no facilities or sites.

The Northern Conservation Zone

are a number of routes to Monteverde, most via the Interamericana, but all are tough and challenging, particularly in the wet season, when 4WD vehicles are essential. It has often been suggested that the road to Monteverde should be paved, but this has always been resisted by local residents, who see the increased number of visitors that would result as a threat to the already fragile environment of the area.

Although synonymous with the famous Cloud Forest Reserve, Monteverde is actually quite a complex area. All routes pass through the village of Santa Elena, to the north of which is the Santa Elena Cloud Forest Reserve, much less visited than Monteverde, but equally rewarding. To the southeast is the straggling Quaker settlement of Monteverde, with numerous dairy farms set back from the road. The entrance to the Cloud Forest Reserve is at the end of the road at the top of the hill.

Monteverde Area

N

| 0 | 400 m |
| 0 | 400 yd |

Santa Elena

FINCA LOS VERDE
EL SAPO DORADO
Clinic
Cerro Plano
PENSION FLOR DE MONTEVERDE
Serpentarium
Bull Ring (Plaza de Toros)
HELICONIA
Monteverde Cloud Forest Reserve
Restaurante de Lucia
EL ESTABLO
MONTEVERDE LODGE
PENSION MANAKIN
CABAÑAS
BELMAR
DE MONTAÑA
LOS PINOS
MONTEVERDE
Centro Panamericano de Idiomas
PENSION EL PINO
Monteverde Conservation League
Monteverde Butterfly Farm
Quebrada Máquina
MONTEVERDE INN
Quebrada
CABINAS EL BOSQUE
La Lecheria (Cheese Factory)
Río Guacimal
Bajo Tigre Trail
Río Guacimal
Monteverde
PENSION FLOR MAR
Friend's Meeting House
FONDA VELA
VILLA VERDE
Footpath
Tilarán
Cordillera de Tilarán
Reserva Ecológica and Hummingbird Gallery
San José

Magical Cloud Forest

Most visitors are captivated by the magical atmosphere of a cloud forest, with its eerie wetness and the echoing calls of birds. The cloud forests of Monteverde and Santa Elena are formed by the Northeast Trade winds; having blown off the Caribbean Sea, the winds then rise over the central mountains of Costa Rica, condensing at the colder levels and forming persistent cloud. The near 100% humidity results in an all-pervading biomass, with vegetation at all levels. There are few surfaces that are not covered in mosses, lichens and epiphytes such

Monteverde Cloud Forest Reserve

as orchids and bromeliads. To walk through the forest is to experience a strange wet half-light, its silence broken by the occasional echoing call of birds or the scurrying of a mammal in the undergrowth.

Monteverde Cloud Forest Reserve

This is a private reserve that was set up in 1972 with the aim of protecting the watershed above the village. More land has been added over the years, so that it now covers around 17,000ha (42,000 acres). The cloud forest reserve covers six life zones and contains a staggering amount of wildlife. Consider these amazing statistics:

• Over 400 species of birds have been recorded, including the Resplendent Quetzal, Three-wattled Bellbird, Bare-necked Umbrellabird and over 30 types of hummingbird.
• 490 species of butterfly have been identified, including the huge Blue Morpho, the Giant Swallowtail, Clearwings and the Zebra Longwing.
• There are over 100 species of mammals, such as monkeys, Baird's Tapir and all six endangered cats found in Costa Rica – Jaguar, Jaguarundi, Puma, Tigrillo, Margay and Ocelot.
• 120 species of reptiles and amphibians have been recorded. The famous Monteverde Golden Toad was discovered here in 1964, but is now feared to be extinct.
• There are an estimated 2500 species of plants.
• More than 6000 species of insects have been identified.

Despite this plethora of wildlife, many visitors complain that they have been disappointed in the number of species that they have seen, largely because of the dense vegetation cover. The answer is to hire one of the excellent local guides, who can be booked at local hotels or at the reserve office.

There is an information centre and gift shop at the entrance to the reserve, where details and maps can be obtained covering the reserve's nine trails (*senderos*), which vary in length from 200m (218yd) to 4km (2.5 miles). Remember that the cloud forest can be both wet and cool, which means that the trails can be very muddy, especially in the wetter parts of the year. Rubber boots

Monteverde Area Top Ten

Resplendent Quetzal
Bare-necked Umbrellabird
Three-wattled Bellbird
Baird's Tapir
Jaguar and other forest cats
Butterflies, including the Blue
  Morpho and Giant Swallowtail
Epiphytes – orchids and bromeliads
Howler Monkey
Agouti
Coati

Monteverde Cloud Forest Reserve

Location: 6km (3.7 miles) southeast of Santa Elena.
Size: 17,000ha (42,000 acres).
Altitude: Straddles the continental divide at 1440m (4662ft).
Getting There: Daily buses from Santa Elena.
Of Interest: Cloud forest, including six life zones, with a staggering amount of fauna and flora.

Quakers

The Quaker movement or the Society of Friends was started in England in the 17th century by George Fox. After the persecution of non-conformist sects, many Quakers moved to America. One group, led by William Penn, founded the colony of Pennsylvania. Pacifism has always been a cornerstone of Quaker belief and in Alabama, in the 1950s, a number of Quakers who had been imprisoned for refusing the draft decided to move to Costa Rica, having been impressed by the country's decision to abolish the army. They settled at Monteverde, where they began dairy farming and cheese making. Visitors to the area will find that the influence of the Quakers (known as *cuáquers* in Costa Rica) is unobtrusive but strong. There is little in the way of entertainment in the evenings and bars, clubs and discos are largely non-existent.

and ponchos can be hired at the reserve and at several of the hotels in the village; also take warm clothing.

The reserve is open 07:00–16:00 daily, but note that only 100 people are allowed into the reserve at any one time and there may be some waiting, especially during the peak hours of 08:00–10:00 in the dry season. Tickets, however, may be booked one day in advance.

The Resplendent Quetzal

Most birders come to Monteverde hoping to see the Resplendent Quetzal (*Pharomachrus mocinno*) – not surprising really, as this is often held to be the most beautiful, but elusive, bird in the Western Hemisphere. The species is 36cm (14in) long, but the males have a tail streamer 64cm (25in) in length. Resplendent Quetzals have an iridescent green body and a red breast, with the wing coverts having a frilled appearance. In addition, the male has a helmet-like crest. Little wonder then that the Resplendent Quetzal has been considered divine throughout history. Many rulers of ancient Central American civilizations, such as the Mayas and Aztecs, wore headdresses made from quetzal feathers. Even today, neighbouring Guatemalans so revere the quetzal that they have chosen it as their national bird.

Resplendent Quetzals can be seen at Monteverde between January and July, starting their breeding in March. They nest in holes in dead trees 3–20m (10–60ft) above the ground and lay two blue eggs, incubated by both the male and female.

Quetzals feed on wild avocado fruit (regurgitating the seed, which helps in the dispersal of the plant), small reptiles, frogs and insects. The main predators, particularly of the young, are squirrels, toucanets, owls and Brown Jays. About 100 monogamous pairs of Resplendent Quetzals nest at Mondeverde. One of the best places to see them is at the start of the Nuboso trail, but the best bet is to employ the services of a local guide.

Accommodation

There is a small amount of budget accommodation in Santa Elena, but mainly mid-range hotels and lodges.

Santa Elena Cloud Forest Reserve

Hotel Belmar, Monteverde, tel: 2469 9091, www.belmar
monteverde.com Swiss-style hotel with valley views from the
balconies.
Monteverde Lodge, Monteverde, tel: 2257 0766,
www.monteverdelodge.com Arguably Monteverde's best
hotel, with transportation to the reserves.
Hotel Finca los Verde, between Santa Elena and Monteverde,
tel: 2645 5157. Tranquil rural setting with basic cabins, restaurant
and horse rentals.

Santa Elena Cloud Forest Reserve

Opened in 1992, Santa Elena is another private reserve and its
administrators give a percentage of its profits to local schools. It is
located 5km (3 miles) north of the village of Santa Elena and
covers an area of 310ha (766 acres) – it is hoped that more forest
will be added soon. It consists of 83% primary forest, with the
remainder being mature secondary forest. It is higher and wetter

*Left: The rare Resplendent
Quetzal is considered by many
to be one of the most beautiful
birds in the world and a
magnet for all bird-watchers
visiting Costa Rica.
Monteverde is as good a place
as any to see this star bird.*

The Northern Conservation Zone

El Bosque Eterno de los Niños

Adjoining the Monteverde Cloud Forest is the **Children's Eternal Rain Forest** established in 1988 after an initiative by Swedish schoolchildren to save forests. It is administered by the Monteverde Conservation League and the amount of forest grows yearly (currently 22,000ha/54,362 acres) as donations pour in from around the world. At the moment there is just one trail, but more are planned in the future.

than Monteverde, but with a similar assemblage of wildlife. However, as the reserve receives fewer visitors, more birds and animals are likely to be seen. There are 10km (6 miles) of trails of varying length and condition, with two miradors giving superb views of Volcán Arenal if the weather is clear. There is a good chance of seeing a Resplendent Quetzal, while mammals include deer, sloths, Ocelots, Howler and Capuchin Monkeys, plus Spider Monkeys, which are not resident at Monteverde. There is a well-organized visitors' centre at the entrance to the reserve, where rubber boots can be hired. The reserve also has a canopy tour, with pulleys and cables running between platforms. This is very exciting, but you probably won't see much wildlife.

Epiphytes

There are over 15,000 types of epiphytes in the tropics. The term describes a plant which, like a parasite, lives on a host (usually a tree). Unlike a parasite, it takes no nutrients from the tree, but relies on rainfall, the air and material from tree branches. As the guides like to say, 'It lives ON the tree, but not OFF it'. In fact, the word 'epiphyte' derives from the Greek *epi* (meaning 'upon') and *phyton* (meaning 'plant'). Epiphytes are found throughout the rainforests of Costa Rica, but thrive particularly in the cloud forests above 1000m (3000ft). The better-known types of

Other Attractions at Monteverde

epiphyte include ferns, lichens, mosses, bromeliads and orchids. Some types of bromeliads form an ecosystem in themselves. Their upturned leaves can hold several litres of water, providing a drinking supply for canopy animals and a habitat for many species to use as shelter and to breed. Some frogs, such as the Poison Arrow Frog, deposit their tadpoles in this water, where they feed upon insect larvae. Some epiphytic plants begin their lives high in the forest canopy and send down long roots that overpower a host tree, eventually killing it. These types of epiphytes eventually become free-standing trees and are known as hemiphytes – a good example is the strangler fig.

Other Attractions at Monteverde

The Hummingbird Gallery beside the entrance to the Monteverde reserve has exhibitions with a wildlife flavour. Outside is a range of feeders which attract hummingbirds, including the Violet Sabrewing, Costa Rica's largest.

The Monteverde Butterfly Farm near Santa Elena is unlike most other butterfly farms in Costa Rica, in that it concentrates on research instead of the export of pupae. Visitors are given a quick lecture and are then taken on a tour of the farm, visiting the greenhouses, where the butterflies are reared, and the screened garden (Jardín de Mariposas), where a large range of butterflies can be seen on the wing. An additional novel feature is the glass-fronted display of a Leaf-cutter Ant colony.

Canopy Tours

Sky Trek is a canopy adventure with a system of trails, suspension bridges, zip lines and platforms. More wildlife is likely to be seen in a more leisurely way at Skywalk, which was built in the canopy of the Monteverde Cloud Forest. The tour includes 2.5km (1.6 miles) of trails and six suspended bridges across deep canyons at the level of the treetops. Biologists now recognize that 90% of all organisms in a rainforest are found in the canopy. This is because the sun rarely reaches the forest floor, but bounces off the canopy fuelling the photosynthesis that results in a plethora of leaves, fruit and seed, providing food for a variety of birds, animals and insects, which can all be viewed with ease from the canopy tour. For details, visit www.monteverdeinfo.com

Monteverde Conservation League

This is a non-profit-making organization founded in 1988, which is gradually buying back deforested land from local farmers. At the same time it is advising farmers about alternative means to make a living. For example, they train locals to become naturalist guides. The League also has an educational role, taking youngsters into the forest for natural history lessons and promoting community awareness. It also has a hands-on role in administering the Children's Eternal Rain Forest.

Opposite: Walkers enjoy a trail in the Monteverde Cloud Forest, where the Resplendent Quetzel is one of over 400 species of birds that have been recorded.

GUANACASTE CONSERVATION ZONE

Costa Rica's northwesterly province of Guanacaste has characteristics that set it apart from the remainder of the country. It is bounded on the east by the volcanic Cordillera de Tilarán and the lower-lying (but equally volcanic) Cordillera de Guanacaste. In the northeast of the region is a line of perfectly shaped volcanoes, including Santa María (1916m/6286ft), Rincón de la Vieja (1895m/6217ft) and Orisí (1487m/4878ft), offering exciting hiking trails. To the west is the Pacific Ocean, with a number of turtle-nesting beaches.

Guanacaste is both the hottest and driest part of the country, the dry season lasting longer than in other provinces. The landscape of much of the province resembles the African Savanna lands, with grasslands and scattered trees and forests. Much of the woodland, however, has been cleared for cattle ranching, giving rise to the description of the area as Costa Rica's 'wild west'. Mounted on their horses, local cowboys or *sabaneros* are a common sight along the roads of Guanacaste.

Guanacaste Top Ten

Minor volcanic features
Capuchin, Howler and Spider Monkeys
Agouti
White-tailed Deer
Variegated Squirrels
Peccaries
Tapirs
White-throated Magpie-Jays
70 species of bat
Wide range of butterflies

Opposite, top to bottom:
Pallas' Long-tongued Bat (Glassophaga soricina) flying out of a cave entrance in the Santa Rosa National Park; a White-tailed Deer, commonly found in the dry forest areas of eastern Costa Rica; horses at Hacienda Guachipelin Lodge in the ranching country of Guanacaste province.

Guanacaste Conservation Zone

Santa Rosa National Park

Santa Rosa National Park

Location: In Guanacaste province, northwestern Costa Rica.
Size: 50,000ha (123,500 acres).
Altitude: Sea level to 500m (1640ft).
Of Interest: Tropical dry forest; turtle nesting beaches; mangroves.

Santa Rosa was designated as a National Park in 1971 – one of the first in the country. With the addition of the Murciélago section on the northern flank, it is also one of the country's largest parks, covering nearly 50,000ha (123,500 acres). Santa Rosa has more cultural, historical and geological interest than most other national parks. The rocks on the Santa Elena peninsula, for example, are amongst the oldest in Costa Rica, dating back some 130 million years to the Cretaceous period. Santa Rosa is the site of three battles in which invaders have been driven out of the country. The first, and the most famous, was in 1856, when the American filibuster William Walker and his men were routed at the Casona Santa Rosa, from which the park gets its name. The battle is said to have lasted a mere 14 minutes! The second battle occurred in 1919 against the Nicaraguans and the third was in 1955, when the Nicaraguan dictator Somoza was put to flight. This is the sum total of Costa Rica's recent military history, which gives an indication of how peaceful the country has been. The *casona* was a working hacienda until the park was established, but it is now a visitors' centre and small museum. All the rooms of the *casona* are open to the public and there are exhibitions of firearms, ecology and a mock-up of a typical rustic kitchen.

Below: Most of the woodland in Guanacaste is of the dry forest variety, losing its leaves during the dry winter months.

Tropical Dry Forest

The ecology of the park is equally interesting. Santa Rosa protects what is believed to be the largest remaining stand of tropical dry forest in Central America. The climate is typified by high temperatures, low precipitation and a long dry season lasting from December to April. This ecosystem consists of a canopy often 30m (100ft) in height, with an understorey of 5–10m (16–33ft) and a typically bare forest floor. During the dry season most plants lose their

Santa Rosa National Park

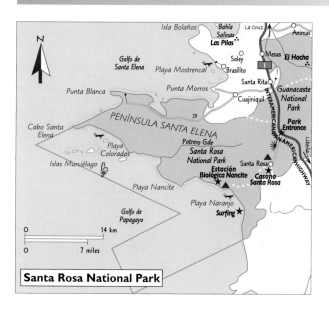

Santa Rosa National Park

leaves, growth slows and flowers and fruit are produced. It is during this season that the wildlife becomes particularly active. Many of the streams dry up at this time, leaving a few water holes where wildlife congregates. Another interesting feature of the dry forest trees and plants is that many of them have spines and thorns. The American biologist Dr Daniel Janzen has suggested that this is a defence mechanism evolved in previous geological times to protect the plants from huge herbivores such as giant sloths and mastodons that were common in this area. Whatever the explanation, hikers should take care – these thorns are sharp!

During the dry season, because of the lack of vegetation, wildlife viewing becomes much easier than in the tropical rainforests. Amongst the mammals, Santa Rosa has White-tailed Deer, Agouti, Armadillos, Capuchin, Howler and Spider Monkeys, Variegated Squirrels, Tapirs, Peccaries, and with luck you might see Pumas, which are believed to be increasing in number in the park. Iguanas are easy to spot and there are 70 species of bat, including Long-tongued Bats, which roost in the eaves of the casona. Birds are prolific (over 250 species) and colourful and include White-throated Magpie-Jays, Orange-fronted Parakeets,

Guanacaste Conservation Zone

Grey-necked Wood-Rail, Turquoise-browed Motmot and Scaly-breasted Hummingbird. There is a vast range of butterflies, including the Blue Morpho, Marpesia and Charaxinae.

Trails through the forest lead to two beaches. Naranjo is a famous surfing beach, while Playa Nancite is an important nesting site for Olive Ridley sea turtles. During *arribadas* in September and October as many as 10,000 turtles can be seen on the beach. There are also stretches of mangroves.

Getting There

From San José, take the Pan-American Highway to Liberia. From there, public buses go to the main gate.

Accommodation

There is no accommodation in the park, except some dormitory beds at Playa Nancite. There's a small camping ground at Playa Naranjo and three other rather primitive sites within the park. Otherwise, use lodges in the Liberia area.

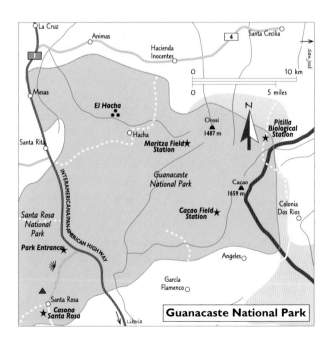

Guanacaste National Park

Guanacaste National Park

The park was set up in 1989, largely due to the input of the American ecologist Dr Daniel Janzen. This huge park covers nearly 80,000ha (197,680 acres) and extends from the Santa Rosa National Park eastwards to the peaks of the Cacao and Orosí volcanoes and over the continental divide onto the Caribbean slopes of these volcanoes. Orosí (1487m/4878ft) is dormant, while the dramatically conical Cacao is notable for the contrast between the rainforest on its eastern slopes and the dry plains on its lower western slopes. It includes a variety of habitats, such as dry forest, rainforest and cloud forest.

When the park was created there were two aims. One was to provide a natural biological corridor to protect the seasonal migratory routes of birds and animals to and from the rainforests in the east and the dry plains in the west. The second aim was to carefully monitor the areas of cattle pasture within the park and as a result aid the natural regeneration of forest.

Fortunately, the park was set up at a time when world beef prices were at a historically low level, so that many of the local farmers were quite willing to sell up their less productive pasture land. Many of the redundant cattlemen have since been trained to work as park personnel.

More research is carried out at Guanacaste than at any other national park in Costa Rica. There are three research stations within the park, located in varying habitats. The Pitilla Biological Station is on the eastern side of Cacao, set amongst rainforest. Cacao Field Station is on the edge of the cloud forest on the southwestern side of Cacao. Maritza Biological Station is further north, between Cacao and Orosí at the junction of the wet and dry forest.

All three research stations offer some primitive accommodation, but access is by dirt roads needing the use of 4WD vehicles. There are few trails and facilities as yet, but the wildlife is outstanding. Mammals include Jaguar, sloths, tapirs and monkeys, while over 300 species of birds have been recorded, many of which move seasonally between the varying habitats.

Guanacaste National Park

Location: Guanacaste province, east of the Pan-American Highway.
Size: 80,000ha (34,800 acres).
Getting There: From Liberia, take the Pan-American Highway north for 42km (29 miles). Turn right opposite the turn-off for Cuajiniquil, and follow the dirt road for 17km (10.5 miles) to the Maritza Biological Station.
Altitude: 200m (820ft) to 1500m (4757ft).
Climate: Hot throughout the year, rainy season from May until November.
Of Interest: Variety of habitats including rainforest, cloud forest, dry tropical forest and dry plains.
Accommodation: Simple dormitory accommodation at the research stations.

CAKARA
(VILLA LAPAS)

ervation Zone

Rincón de la Vieja National Park

Location: In Guanacaste Province, northwestern Costa Rica.
Size: 14,083ha (34,600 acres).
Altitude: From 650m (2132ft) to 1965m (6449ft).
Climate: Hot and wet (2540–5080mm/100–200in of rain annually) on the Caribbean slope. Pronounced dry season from December to March on the Pacific slope. Cool at altitude.
Of Interest: Rainforest, dry tropical forest, volcanic features.

This popular national park covers some 14,000ha (34,600 acres) and is noted for its volcanic features as well as its prolific wildlife. It is named after the Rincón de la Vieja volcano, which rises to 1895m (6217ft) and is spasmodically active. The last major eruption was in 1983, but there was a minor eruption in 1991, causing ash-mud flows which destroyed much of the forest on the southeastern slope. The heat here is close to the surface and there is plenty of peripheral activity to see in the Las Pallas area, with 50ha (124 acres) of hot springs, mud springs, fumeroles and solfataras. The heat has led to one of the largest geothermal electricity generation plants in the world being located here. The name Rincón de la Vieja translates as 'the old lady's corner'. This probably originated with the local Guatuso indigenous tribe, who believed there was an old witch on the summit of the mountain. She was thought to send columns of smoke into the air when she was angry.

The park has six different life zones, with a strong contrast between the east and west slopes. The Caribbean slope is hot and wet and covered with rainforest, while the Pacific side of the Cordillera has a distinct dry season leading to sparser forests. Nearer the summits, the tree growth is stunted due to the cold and wind. The scenery also includes lava flows, a freshwater lake (Los Jilgueros) and a string of waterfalls in the Agria ravine. Three of the waterfalls exceed 70m (230ft) and one has a deep plunge pool, ideal for a refreshing swim. There are a number of trails leading from the two ranger stations, one of which goes to the summit of Rincón de la Vieja – a two-day hike there and back, with the summit likely to be in the clouds and the path marked by cairns. The view from the summit, if it is clear, is rewarding, with Lake Nicaragua glistening in the distance and the Pacific Ocean to the west. The ranger stations are in old *casonas*, one of which was owned by the former US President Lyndon B Johnson.

The wildlife of Rincón de la Vieja National Park is both prolific and diverse. Three species of monkey can be found here – Howler, Spider and Capuchin. Other mammals include sloths, Kinkajous, tapirs and Tayras. The secretive Jaguar has also been seen. More than 300 species of bird have been recorded including

Rincón de la Vieja National Park

Resplendent Quetzals, Great Currasow, numerous parrots and toucans, eagles, trogons and the Three-wattled Bellbird.

Minor Volcanic Activity

Volcanoes are normally associated with explosive activity involving bombs, ash and lava ejected from craters. Few volcanoes are continually active (although Arenal in recent years has been an exception to the rule), and most go through dormant periods. During dormancy, heat often remains close underground, giving rise to hot springs which feed into rivers rich in minerals, which in turn support *balnearios* or health spas, such as Tabacon, near Fortuna. Other features include mud springs (also used for health treatments), fumeroles (which are vents through which steam issues), solfataras (which emit sulphurous gases) and, most spectacular of all, geysers, where hot water is ejected to considerable height at regular intervals. Most of these features can be seen in the Rincón de la Vieja National Park.

Below: Boiling mud pools are among the peripheral volcanic features to be found in the Rincón de la Vieja National Park. Many of the features are easily accessible from footpaths.

Getting There

From Liberia, take the Pan-American Highway north for 5km (3 miles). Turn right at the village of Cereceda and continue on for 23km (14 miles) to the Las Paillas ranger station.

Accommodation

There is a camp site in the park, but no other accommodation, apart from a few bunk beds in the ranger stations. Fortunately there are some good lodges nearby:

Buenavista Lodge, in the hamlet of Cañas Dulces, 35km (22 miles) north of Liberia, tel: 2695 5147. A working cattle ranch, which runs hiking and horse riding tours.

Guanacaste Conservation Zone

Cowboy Culture

A common sight along the roads, tracks and fields of Guanacaste is the cowboy or *sabanero* who works on a cattle farm or *ganadería*. A strong 'cowboy culture' has developed here, which is every bit as evocative as that in the American 'Wild West'. *Sabaneros* are renowned as tough, hard-drinking, skilled men, who live on the horse and confine their wives to the kitchen. Their skills are displayed in the local rodeos and *corridas* held throughout the Guanacaste region. To learn more about *sabaneros*, go to the **Museo del Sabanero**, located in the Casa del Cultura in Liberia. There are many artefacts from the old *casonas* or fortified ranches, including furniture, stoves, branding irons, saddles and rope work.

Hacienda Lodge, Guachipelin Apdo 636, Alajuela, tel: 2441 6545. Another working ranch, offering 25 comfortable rooms plus some basic bunkhouse accommodation that is part of the Costa Rican Youth Hostel system. Hiking and horse riding tours are provided, along with guides.

Howler Monkeys

There are four types of monkey in Costa Rica and the Howler (Alouatta family) is probably the most common, appearing in all three national parks in Guanacaste province. They are the largest of the New World monkeys, ranging in size from 56–92cm (23–36in), excluding the prehensile tail, which can be equally long. Howlers, known as *congos* in Costa Rica, live in groups of about 18 and maintain contact and mark their territory with a loud barking whoop – a call that is one of the loudest in the animal world and which is certainly quite frightening when heard by walkers on forest trails, although they are rarely aggressive to humans. Howlers are the least active of the Costa Rican monkeys, resting for 80% of the time. They live mainly in the

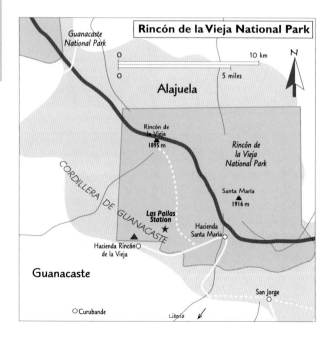

Rincón de la Vieja National Park

Left: Howler Monkeys are the largest and most common of the four species of monkey in Costa Rica. Their call is said to be the loudest in the animal world.

canopy, where they eat leaves, buds, fruit, flowers and nuts. Howlers have few enemies except man, but are vulnerable to loss of habitat. Their lifespan is usually between 15 and 20 years.

The Guanacaste Tree

Guanacaste province gets its name from the Guanacaste tree (*Enterolobium cyclocarpum*), which is the national tree of Costa Rica. Common in Guanacaste province, it is easily recognizable as it expands (greater in width than it does in height), with the lower branches just a few feet from the ground, providing welcome shade for both wild and domestic animals. The boles of the Guanacaste tree are cylindrical and straight, without the buttresses normally seen in tropical trees. It is deciduous and loses its leaves in the dry season from January to March, with buds reappearing in April. It has beautiful white flowers, which are very fragrant, the scent pervading the air for many metres in all directions. The seeds mature in time for the rainy season, which should help in germination. They have hard shells, however, and these are usually ignored by local fauna. Janzen and Martin (1982) believe that the seeds were originally dispersed by creatures that are now extinct, such as giant sloths and mastadons. The wood of the Guanacaste tree is hard and reddish-brown and highly regarded in the furniture industry.

NORTH PACIFIC COASTAL CONSERVATION AREA

The North Pacific coastal area includes part of Guanacaste province and the coastline of the north Nicoya Peninsula. With low rainfall, hot temperatures and ample sunshine even in the wet season, this area has become Costa Rica's holiday playground. Despite the controversial Papagayo Project (which is well on the way to providing the proposed 10,000 rooms, a marina and a golf course), most developments are small scale and tasteful. Nevertheless, the holiday industry is a threat to habitats such as mangroves and turtle-nesting beaches, so that conservation measures have been needed. Access to the area from San José has, until recently, been a long drawn out affair, but the new international airport at Liberia and the recently built Friendship Bridge, which cuts across the marshland at the head of the Tempisque River, have speeded up communications considerably.

North Pacific Top Ten

Leatherback and Olive Ridley Turtles
Brown Pelicans
Magnificent Frigatebird
Endemic birds on Isla del Coco
Raccoons
Coatis
Basilisk Lizards
Lesser Nighthawk
American Oystercatcher
Five species of Mangrove tree

Opposite, top to bottom:
The Brown Pelican (Pelecanus occidentalis) is common along the shores of the North Pacific coast; thousands of Olive Ridley Turtles nest on the beach at the Ostional National Wildlife Refuge; one of many exotic fish to be found on the coral reefs around Costa Rica's coastline.

North Pacific Coastal Conservation Area

Isla Bolaños Biological Reserve

Located in Salinas Bay, close to the Nicaraguan border, this 14ha (35-acre) island and the surrounding marine environment were designated as a wildlife refuge in 1981. The idea was to protect the nest sites of Brown Pelicans and Magnificent Frigatebirds. The island is also the only known nesting site in Costa Rica of the American Oystercatcher. The island is one of the driest and most barren places in the country, which, along with the thin, poor soil, has resulted in a cover of low scrub. Visitors are barred from the island during the nesting season between December and March. Access at other times is by boat from Puerto Soley – a trip of around 3km (1.9 miles).

Brown Pelicans

The Brown Pelican (*Pelecanus occidentalis*) is one of the most recognizable and best-loved of birds. It is actually the smallest of the eight species in the pelican family and differs from the others in that it is entirely marine; it is the only dark pelican and the only one that dives from the air into the water to catch its food. About four feet in length, the Brown Pelican has a brown and grey body and a long greyish-yellow bill with a large pouch of skin. The pouch can hold nearly three gallons of water and fish, which is two to three times what its stomach can contain. It fishes by diving and then using the pouch as a net. It strains the water out of the side of its bill before swallowing the fishes – otherwise the weight of the fish would prohibit the pelican from taking off. Despite their ungainly appearance on land, Brown Pelicans are excellent fliers and will soar on thermals for some considerable time. They are also gregarious birds and are often seen in large groups gliding low over the water in single file or in a V shape – a truly magnificent sight. Brown Pelicans usually nest on islands on the ground. But on Isla Bolaños some 200 pairs nest in the tops of stunted trees. They are unusual in that, unlike most birds, they do not warm their eggs using the skin on their breasts, but incubate using their large webbed feet. Brown Pelicans form no threat to the fishing industry as the fish that they take are rarely caught for human consumption. They are, however, on the endangered list, largely due to the effects of DDT poisoning in the last century. The Costa Rican population appears to be stable or gently increasing.

Las Baulas National Marine Park

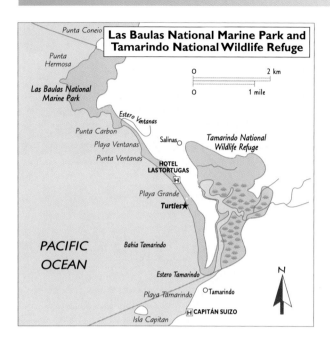

Las Baulas National Marine Park

This marine national park is named after the *baula*, the Giant Leatherback Turtle, which comes ashore here on Playa Grande to lay its eggs between November and March. The 445ha (1099-acre) reserve was set up in 1990 with the express purpose of protecting this nesting site, the most important in Costa Rica. This followed a 15-year battle between developers and conservationists, which ended with compromises on both sides. In the nesting season, however, the beach is sacrosanct. From 15 October to 15 February it is open at night to visitors accompanied by a guide. Groups cannot exceed 15 people and there is a limit of 60 people per night. The tours are preceded by a brief educational presentation at the ranger stations. Tickets include the services of a guide and reservations are mandatory. There are a number of other sensible restrictions – visitors must not get too close to the turtles and flashlights on cameras are not allowed. Unauthorized tours also run from Tamarindo, mainly boat trips run by local boatmen. In addition to the turtles, Playa Grande boasts an outstanding surfing beach, with a good mix of

Las Baulas National Marine Park

Location: On the Pacific coast southwest of Liberia.

Size: 445ha (1100 acres), plus 22,000ha (54,362 acres) of ocean.

Altitude: Sea level.

Climate: Hot throughout the year. Rainy season from May to December.

Of Interest: Giant Leatherback Turtle nesting beach.

North Pacific Coastal Conservation Area

Credit for saving the Giant Leatherback Turtles of Playa Grande and the setting up of the marine national park must largely go to Louis Wilson and Marianel Pastor, owners of the nearby Hotel las Tortugas. In the 1970s a company was taking the turtles' eggs to make biscuits, while the beach was subdivided among numerous poachers, who sold the eggs as an aphrodisiac. Wilson bought the rights from the poachers to take tourists to certain sections of sand and used the poachers as guides. Credit should also go to local resident Maria Koberg, described as 'a one-woman crusade', for educating local schoolchildren and boy scouts to appreciate the turtles and the need for their protection. As a result of the pressure from such local people, the Costa Rican government agreed to declare the area a national park in 1980.

lefts and rights. Sea angling is also outstanding, with marlin and sailfish the main attractions.

Getting There

From the intersection on the Pan-American Highway at Liberia, drive west towards the Pacific coast. At the town of Belén, take the signposted gravel roads for 29km (19 miles) to Salinas and the entrance to the national park.

Accommodation

Hotel Las Tortugas, right on the beach at Playa Grande, tel: 2653 0423. Comfortable rooms with air conditioning. Owned by Louis Wilson, who played a big part in setting up the park.

There are numerous hotels to suit all pockets in Tamarindo, including:

Capitán Suizo, at the southern end of the town, tel: 2653 0075, www.hotelcapitansuizo.com This is the area's luxury option. Freeform pool, luxuriant gardens with resident Howler Monkeys, tours arranged.

Tamarindo Diria, tel: 2653 0031, www.tamarindodiria.com Refurbished luxury hotel. Rooms with ocean and tropical garden views. Excellent poolside restaurant.

Giant Leatherback Turtles

The largest of the world's seven species of sea turtle, the Giant Leatherback (*Dermochelys coriacea*) can average 350kg (110lb) and measure up to 2m (6ft) in length. The largest ever found (on a beach in North Wales) was over 3m (10ft) long and weighed over 900kg (1985lb). Leatherbacks are the reptile world's deepest divers, having been recorded at a depth of 1200m (3600ft). They are found mainly in the open ocean, but often feed in shallow offshore waters if their main prey, the jellyfish, is in abundance. They start their life as hatchlings and are immediately in danger of predation, from birds, reptiles and mammals. Perhaps only 5% reach maturity. Mating takes place at sea and Leatherback males never leave the water. Female Leatherbacks generally return to the same beach on which they were born in order to nest, preferring beaches of soft sand with a shallow approach from the sea. They excavate a nest above the high water line with their flippers, laying

Tamarindo National Wildlife Refuge

Above: *The Leatherback is the largest of the world's sea turtles. Although the adults have few natural predators, their numbers have plummeted in recent years and they are now regarded as endangered.*

between 80 and 100 golf ball-sized eggs, 80% of which will be fertile. The female then back-fills the nest and lumbers back into the sea. The eggs, meanwhile, hatch in about 60 or 70 days. At Playa Grande, the nesting season is from November to March, when females come ashore at high tide at night and will nest as many as 12 times in a season.

Leatherbacks Under Threat

Although adult Leatherbacks have few natural predators, the activities of man pose a serious threat. There is little demand for their flesh as compared with other sea turtles, but their nests are regularly raided for their eggs and the turtles are often caught in the nets of commercial fishing vessels. Pollution can also be a problem and many turtles die from consuming plastic bags, which resemble jellyfish, their main food. It is also claimed that Leatherbacks can become disorientated by the bright lights of holiday resorts when they are attempting to return to their nesting sites. Clearly the Giant Leatherback is classified as an endangered species and the following figures from Playa Grande support this: in 1989/90 over 1300 leatherbacks nested on the beach; by 2000/01 the figure had dropped to 363, and in 2003/04 the total had plummeted to 159. Because the Leatherback (and indeed other sea turtles) is migratory by nature, an international response is necessary for effective conservation.

Tamarindo National Wildlife Refuge

This small reserve of 385ha (953 acres) is now part of Las Baulas National Marine Park. It was originally set up in 1990 to protect a mangrove swamp that is unusual in having no freshwater input for nearly half the year, the creeks that feed the Matapalo estuary drying up completely from December to April. Five species of mangrove can be seen in the estuary and when the tide is out, the

North Pacific Coastal Conservation Area

Above: The mangroves in the Tamarindo estuary provide a home for numerous birds, mammals and mud crabs. In many areas, the mangroves form the first line of defence against coastal erosion.

protruding vertical roots (or pneumataphores) can be seen sticking out of the mud – this helps to aerate the plants. Life in the mangroves is varied, with some 57 species of birds, including Great Egret, Cattle Egret and Blue Heron. An unusual species here is the nocturnal Lesser Nighthawk (related to the European Nightjar and the North American Whip-poor-will), which spends the daylight hours lying camouflaged on the mangrove branches. Howler Monkeys are sure to be heard and there is a good chance of seeing White-faced Monkeys, Raccoons, Basilisk Lizards and Caiman. Crabs can be seen scurrying around the mud. Boats may be hired at Tamarindo to tour the mangroves – early morning is the best time to see the most species.

Mangroves

Mangroves are trees that grow in saline coastal habitats in the tropics and subtropics. They are able to exploit their habitat by developing physiological adaptations to overcome the problems of high salinity and frequent tidal inundation. There are five species of mangrove in Costa Rica – the Black Mangrove, the White Mangrove, the Red Mangrove, Tea Mangrove and Buttonwood Mangrove. All are found at Tamarindo, with the red being the most common. Each type of mangrove has different environmental requirements, so that a clear zoning is often seen. Once established, mangrove roots provide a habitat for oysters, barnacles, sponges and bryozoans. Mangrove crabs thrive in this environment and improve the nutritional quality of the mud by mulching mangrove leaves. The roots slow down tidal flow and encourage the deposition of sediment. Mangroves are often the first line of defence against storm surges and it is claimed that they have prevented loss of life during hurricanes and tsunamis. Although fully protected in Costa Rica, mangrove swamps are

Ostional National Wildlife Refuge

under threat in many parts of the world, particularly from tourist developments and shrimp farming.

Ostional National Wildlife Refuge

The Ostional reserve is located just to the north of the resort of Nosara, based around Playa Ostional. The reserve was created in 1982 with the purpose of protecting the nesting grounds of the Olive Ridley marine turtle (*Lepidochalys olivacea*), known in Costa Rica as the *loro*. Although the Olive Ridley nests here throughout the year (as do Leatherbacks and Green Turtles at other times), the best time to visit Ostional is before and during *arribadas* (literally 'arrivals'), when the turtles come ashore in their thousands, making this one of the most amazing ecological experiences in Costa Rica. The best months are between July and December at the start of the last quarter of the moon. The *arribada* begins with a few hundred Olive Ridleys coming ashore, and then others follow in their thousands for the next few days. The largest *arribada* recorded at Ostional was in November 1995, when it was calculated that over 500,000 females came ashore. At times the beach is completely covered with the turtles, their flippers throwing sand everywhere and slapping the shells of neighbours. Inevitably, many of the earlier nests are destroyed by latecomers. Hatchlings are given some protection as they return to the sea, where the surviving females will remain for around 10 years before returning to their home beach to nest.

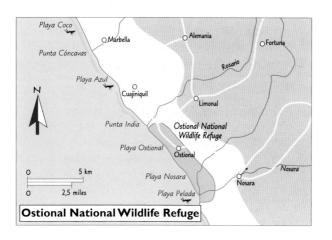

Ostional National Wildlife Refuge

North Pacific Coastal Conservation Area

Egg poaching has also been a time-honoured tradition in the area – the eggs are widely used in cooking. Raccoons, Coatis and other mammals also take a heavy toll, so that it is reckoned that only one per cent of the eggs will hatch. Hatchlings have to run the gauntlet of Frigatebirds and other sea birds, plus predators in the sea. The upshot was that the Olive Ridley was unable to maintain its population.

In 1987, scientists initiated a project allowing the local people to harvest a percentage of the eggs from the first three days of the *arribada*. Many of these eggs would, of course, have been destroyed by the turtles themselves. Thereafter, the locals protect the remaining nests. The idea is to deter poaching and at the same time help the local economy. By this method, it is estimated that the survival rate of the eggs has risen to eight per cent.

The Ostional National Wildlife Refuge covers 352ha (869 acres) of land reserve and 8000ha (19,767 acres) of marine zone. The beach is backed by sparse dry forest with a healthy population of Howler and Capuchin Monkeys. The Nosara River mouth is surrounded by mangrove swamps with crocodiles and around 100 species of birds. Canoes may be hired to explore the mangroves.

Treasure Island

For centuries the Isla del Coco was the haunt of pirates and buccaneers – it is often claimed that it was the inspiration for Robert Louis Stevenson's *Treasure Island*. These pirates were said to have buried treasure on the island. There is, in fact, a supposedly authentic 'treasure map'. Many expeditions have attempted to find the treasure, but have always been unsuccessful. Unfortunately, it was these expeditions that brought in the introduced mammals that have devastated the indigenous wildlife.

Magnificent Frigatebirds

A frequent predator of turtle hatchlings is the Magnificent Frigatebird (*Fregata magnificens*). Common along the Pacific coast, it is large – some 100cm (39in) long, with a 215cm (85in) wingspan – and mainly black in colour, although the male has a scarlet throat pouch that can be inflated in the breeding season. The female has a white breast and a blue eye ring. It is an elegant flier with a long forked tail and will soar for hours in thermals.

Magnificent Frigatebirds feed on the wing, plucking flying fish, jellyfish and squids from the sea and turtle hatchlings from the beach. They also concentrate around fishing boats and fish docks, where they feed on offal. Oddly for a marine bird, it cannot swim, as its long, narrow wings would find it difficult to lift the bird from the water. Magnificent Frigatebirds practise kleptparasitism – stealing food from other birds by chasing them in the air until they disgorge their meal. They will also steal nesting material

Isla del Coco National Park

from other birds. They are sometimes known as 'Man-O'-War birds', due, no doubt, to their piratical nature.

Isla del Coco National Park

Some 523km (330 miles) to the southwest of the Nicoya Peninsula is Cocos Island, claimed to be the largest uninhabited island in the world. Covering 2400ha (5930 acres) and rising to 634m (6348ft), it represents the tip of an ancient volcano and is covered with luxuriant rainforest. In many ways it resembles the Galapagos in that it has a large number of endemic species, many of which evolved after their arrival, changing into distinct forms that are found nowhere else in the world. Among these endemics are two species of small lizards, 65 insects, various fishes and three birds – the Cocos Flycatcher, the Cocos Cuckoo and the Cocos Finch – the latter of which is related to the Darwins Finches of the Galapagos. Unfortunately, there are other creatures introduced by man, who has brought in pigs, goats and white-tailed deer with the hope of providing fresh meat on return trips. Rats and cats, too, have escaped from boats and these non-native animals can cause considerable damage to the existing flora and fauna of the island. The most frequent visitors to the Isla del Coco today are divers, who appreciate the clear waters, the pristine coral reef and water creatures such as whales and the generally harmless hammerhead shark.

Isla del Coco National Park

Location: 523km (330 miles) from mainland Costa Rica.

Size: 2400ha (5930 acres).

Altitude: Sea level, rising to 634m (6348ft).

Climate: Hot and wet. Average temperature 24°C (75°F), average rainfall 6000mm (240in)

Of Interest: Endemic birds, insects and fish; pristine coral reef; tropical rainforest.

Getting There: Cocos Island is about 30 hours from the mainland by boat. Charters and diving tours are the only practical options for visitors.

Accommodation: None on the island. Most visitors stay on boats.

Isla del Coco National Park

SOUTH NICOYA/TEMPISQUE CONSERVATION AREA

The Nicoya Peninsula is one of the hottest and driest parts of Costa Rica and its shoreline, with sandy beaches interspersed with headlands, supports a number of small resorts. The area has always been hampered in its development by a poor infrastructure, but the building of the new Friendship Bridge across the Tempisque swamplands has improved communications to the northern part of the area. The south of the peninsula is usually reached by ferry from Puntarenas or by air from the capital San José to the new resort of Tambor. There are a number of parks and reserves in the area. Between the regional capital of Nicoya and the Tempisque River is the Barra Honda National Park, unusual in that it is based on a limestone area with many underground features. To the east, the swamplands and forest on the Tempisque flood plain are protected in the Palo Verde National Park, which is rich in bird life. The south coast of the Nicoya Peninsula boasts two excellent reserves: Curú National Wildlife Refuge is a small privately owned reserve based on a working hacienda, while the Cabo Blanco Absolute Nature Reserve occupies the whole of the southwest tip of the peninsula, with dry tropical forest and breeding sea birds.

Palo Verde Top Ten

Jabiru Stork
Black-crowned Night Heron
Roseate Spoonbill
White Ibis
Wood Stork
Scarlet Macaw
Crocodiles
Peccaries
Howler and Capuchin Monkeys
Coatis

Opposite, top to bottom:
A female Ruby-throated
Hummingbird, the most
widespread of Costa Rica's 50+
hummers; the Blue Morpho, the
most spectacular Costa Rican
butterfly; a Laughing Gull –
these are common in the winter,
but they are mainly immature
birds who do not have the
distinctive black cap.

South Nicoya/Tempisque Conservation Area

Barra Honda National Park

Barra Honda National Park

Location: Midway between Nicoya and the Tempisque River.
Size: 2295ha (5670 acres).
Altitude: Up to 442m (1450ft).
Climate: Hot in the dry season, hot and humid in the wet season.
Of interest: Underground limestone features; dry tropical forest.
Getting There: From San José, take the Pan-American Highway to the turn-off for the new Friendship (Tempisque) Bridge. Cross the bridge, continue for 13km (8 miles), then turn right to Barra Honda. Follow the signs to the park entrance and ranger station (open 08:00 till dusk, tel: 2671 1062 for permits).

Volcano?

Until the middle of the last century, it was believed that Barra Honda was a volcano. A depression on the top of the main ridge was thought to be a crater and out of it came noises likened to a steam engine, along with a foul smell. As the cave system was thoroughly explored, it was soon realised that Barra Honda was not formed by vulcanicity. The noise came from the wings of tens of thousands of bats, while the smell emanated from their accumulated droppings.

The park covers some 2295ha (5670 acres) at the surface, but it is the underground features that attract visitors. There is a complex of caves and caverns dating back some 70 million years. More than 40 caves have been discovered to date, with many more awaiting exploration. The caves vary in depth from just a few feet to over 240m (787ft) and often require a vertical descent. For this reason, advance application is required to explore the caves, along with climbing gear and the services of a guide. The caves display a full range of limestone features, such as stalactites, stalagmites, pillars and flow structures. They are formed in the following way: rain is a weak acid that can dissolve limestone rocks leaving caves and caverns underground. The lime-rich water also seeps through joints in the rock into the caves where it re-deposits the lime, forming the dripstone features we see at Barra Honda. Santa Ana is the deepest cave, descending to 240m (787ft).

Some of the caves are occupied by bats, including *Pozo Hediondo*, or Fetid Pit Cave, named after the smell of the accumulated bat droppings. Most visitors enter through Torciopelo Cave, named after the dead snake found there when it was first explored. This cave has some of the best features in the complex, including The Organ, the flutes of which produce musical sounds when gently tapped. Nicoa Cave has revealed remains of pre-Columbian people, along with utensils believed to be over 2000 years old.

Above ground, there is a network of hiking trails through dry tropical forest. You are bound to hear Howler Monkeys and, with luck, spot White-tailed Deer, Raccoons, Peccaries, Anteaters, Kinkajous and Agoutis. Scarlet Macaws are also reputed to nest near here.

Accommodation

There is a camp site in the park. Most visitors stay in Nicoya:
Hotel Jenny, 200m south of Parque Central, tel: 2685 5050. An old house with large rooms, with cabinas at the rear.

Hotel Curime, on the road to Playa Sámara, tel: 2685 5238. Twenty cabins in pleasing landscaped grounds. Swimming pool.

Palo Verde National Park

Palo Verde National Park

At the head of the Gulf of Nicoya lies the flood plain of the
Tempisque River. This area is now protected by the Palo Verde

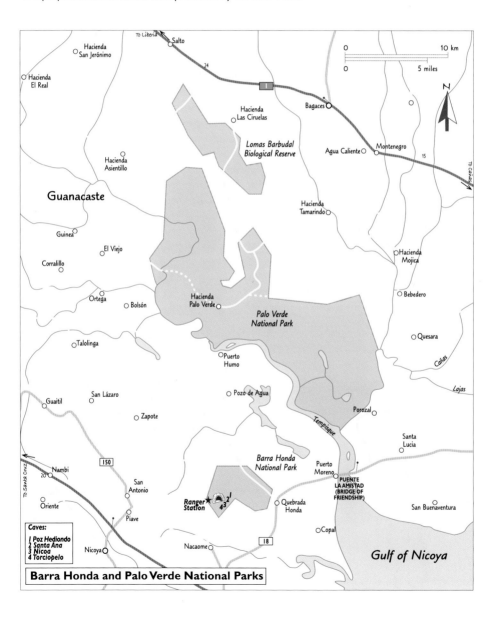

Barra Honda and Palo Verde National Parks

South Nicoya/Tempisque Conservation Area

Palo Verde National Park

Location: Guanacaste Province, at the head of the Gulf of Nicoya.

Size: 17,000ha (42,000 acres).

Altitude: Sea level to 200m (656ft).

Climate: Hot and humid in the wet season. It can be extremely hot in the dry season (this is one of the warmest parts of the country, so take plenty of water and sun block).

Of Interest: One of the best wetlands in Costa Rica. There are mangroves and dry tropical forest, full of bird life, reptiles and mammals.

Below: A ~~female~~ *juvenile* *Black-crowned Night Heron. This species is common in the lowlands around the Gulf of Nicoya.*

National Park, which also incorporates the Lomas Barbudal Bilogical Reserve and the Dr Rafael Lucas Rodríguez Caballero National Wildlife Refuge. Now covering 17,000ha (42,000 acres), the park boasts twelve habitats, including freshwater and saltwater lagoons, marsh and swamp, pastureland, black mangroves and deciduous and evergreen dry tropical forest, making it one of the most varied national parks in Costa Rica. Over 150 types of trees have been recorded, including the *Palo Verde* (or Horse Bean) meaning 'green tree' – the leaves, branches and even the trunk are green in colour. Geologically, the park is also interesting, with low ridges of limestone and both sedimentary and volcanic rocks.

During the wet season, the lowland is flooded with water from the Tempisque and Bebedero rivers, plus tidal flows from the Gulf (the tidal range is up to 4m/13ft). In the dry season, the waters shrink back to scattered pools. The whole area is a bird-watcher's paradise, with over 300 species recorded. It is the dry season that is most attractive to birders. The birds concentrate on the remaining wet areas, while at the same time many of the trees have lost their leaves, making it easier to spot wildlife. In addition, there are fewer mosquitoes and bugs in the dry season. It is estimated that over a quarter of a million wading birds and wildfowl, many from North America, spend the winter months here. Among the resident species are some of the country's larger, more exotic birds, such as the stunning Roseate Spoonbill, Anhinga, White Ibis, Wood Stork, Great Egret, Black-bellied Whistling Duck and Northern Jacana. You may also see the Jabiru, the largest stork in the New World. The main nesting area is an island in the middle of the Tempisque River, known as the Isla de Pájaros. This is home to the country's largest colony of Black-crowned Night Herons. The river supports a large number of crocodiles, which loaf on the sandbanks. The dry forest areas are rich in mammal life and the visitor should see Howler

Palo Verde National Park

and Capuchin Monkeys, Coatis, Peccaries, White-tailed Deer and Variegated Squirrels.

The park headquarters are based at the old Hacienda Palo Verde (tel: 2671 1290), and are operated by the Organization of Tropical Studies. Three well-maintained trails lead from the station through the forest to lookout points over the river and marshland. There is a small dock near to the administration centre, where boats may be hired to view the Isla de Pájaros – note that landing is not permitted.

A word of warning: Palo Verde is noted for its variety of bees, most of which are harmless. An exception to the rule is the Africanized Bee, which has recently colonized the area. These are extremely aggressive and will actively pursue anyone who disturbs their nests.

Getting There
Leave the Pan-American Highway at the town of Bagaces and turn west on a gravel road that leads for 19km (12 miles) to the park entrance. It is a further 9 km (6 miles) to the administration centre.

Accommodation
No accommodation in the park itself. The nearest option is **La Ensenada Lodge**, 20km (12.5 miles) west of the Punta Morales junction on the Pan-American Highway, tel: 2223 6653. A working hacienda; simple cabins with air conditioning and private facilities.

Hummingbirds
There are 330 species of New World hummingbirds, of which over 50 occur in Costa Rica, where they can be found from sea level to the top of the highest mountains – indeed, anywhere there are nectar-filled flowers, which are their major source of nourishment. They are usually brightly coloured and often iridescent and characterized by their small size, some being little bigger than a bumble bee. They have a variety of bill sizes and shapes, which have adapted to the type of flower from which they obtain their nectar. Hummingbirds are remarkable fliers, the bones in their wings allowing them to beat up 80 times per second, to hover and even fly backwards. They have the fastest metabolism of any

The Chorotegas

The Nicoya Peninsula was the stronghold of Costa Rica's most advanced *indigenas* group, the Chorotegas. It is believed that the Chorotegas were the country's only *indigenas* race to have a written language. Their spoken language was akin to that of the Maya and Aztec people further north. It was social upheaval in this area that forced the Chorotegas south to the Nicoya Peninsula around AD800. It appears that they had a belief system that involved blood-letting and the sacrifice of animals and humans. Their economy was based on the growing of maize and they also cultivated tobacco, fruit and cotton, while their currency was the cacao bean. Although they were skilled artisans, working in jade and gold, they are best known today, however, for their pottery. The skill declined during the Spanish Conquest, but there has been a recent revival using similar raw materials, based on archaeological research. The pottery is traditionally coloured black, red and white and decorated with animal motifs. Today, the pottery workers are mainly women and their work can be observed in the village of Guatil near Nicoya.

South Nicoya/Tempisque Conservation Area

The Cabo Blanco Reserve was created in 1963 by Olaf Wessberg, a Swede, and his Danish wife, Karen Morgenson, after making a worldwide appeal for funds to buy the land. It is, in fact, the oldest piece of protected land in Costa Rica and was donated to the nation long before a national park system came into existence. Wessberg, who has been described as the 'father of the National Park system', took on many environmental causes, but was murdered in the Osa Peninsula (reportedly by logging interests) while looking at the possibility of establishing another national park there. A plaque near the Cabo Blanco ranger station has been erected in his honour. His wife, Karen, went on to become one of Costa Rica's leading environmentalists. She died in 1994.

Cabo Blanco Top Ten

Brown Booby
Monkeys
Armadillo
Margay
Ocelot
Sun Bittern
Motmot
Crested Caracara
Blue Morpho
Anteater

creature. On cold nights they go into a coma-like torpor while sleeping in order not to starve to death. Although they get most of their nourishment from nectar, many species of hummingbird gain protein from insects and spiders. Most will aggressively defend their territories, in which the female will build a small nest often no bigger than an egg cup. Predators include the smaller, more agile hawks, some frogs and large insects like Praying Mantises.

Jabiru Stork

The jabiru is the largest of the stork family and the tallest flying bird found in Central and South America, an adult reaching up to 1.5m (5ft) in height, with a wingspan of 2.8m (9.2ft). It is mostly white in colour, except for the black and featherless neck and head and a red stretchable pouch at the base of the neck. The jabiru forages in freshwater marshes, where it stalks purposefully around. It eats fish, mud eels, molluscs and amphibians, while it will also eat carrion and dead fish, helping to maintain the quality of water. Although ungainly on the ground, the jabiru is a strong and graceful flier, often soaring to great heights. It usually nests in the crown of a mangrove tree during the months of June to September. The Tempisque Basin is the jabiru's only breeding area in Costa Rica, although it is occasionally seen in other wetland areas outside the nesting season. Jabiru numbers are thought to be declining, but it is not considered highly endangered.

Cabo Blanco Absolute Nature Reserve

The reserve occupies 1175ha (2903 acres) of forest at the southern tip of the Nicoya Peninsula. It gets its name from an offshore island covered with the white guano of sea birds. The 'absolute' part comes from the fact that for the first 25 years of its existence it was 'absolutely' a nature reserve and nothing else, and no visitors were allowed. The southern part of the peninsula receives more rain (2300mm/58in) than the rest of the area and is characterized by moist tropical forest. About 15% is primary forest, with the remaining secondary forest some 50 years old. Around 150 trees have been identified; evergreen species predominate, but dry forest types are found as well. Among the most common trees are Bastard Cedar, Wild Plum, Gumbo-limbo, Lancewood, Frangipani and Spiny Cedar – the latter has sharp conical spines protruding from the bark and white flowers that

Cabo Blanco Absolute Nature Reserve

are pollinated by bats at night. There is one particularly fine specimen of Spiny Cedar in the reserve: 50m (164ft) in height, with a bole 3m (10ft) in diameter.

The forest is home to a wide variety of animals, including Howler, Capuchin and Spider Monkeys, Agouti, Coati, Armadillos, Anteaters, Collared Peccary, Porcupine and Raccoons. Smaller cats such as Ocelot and Margay leave traces, but are unlikely to be seen. The shoreline is inhabited by many sea birds, such as Brown Pelicans, Laughing Gulls and Frigatebirds, while Cabo Blanco island is the nesting site of up to 800 pairs of Brown Boobies. The forest contains a rich array of birds, such as Magpie-Jay, Motmot, Long-tailed Mannikin, Crested Caracara, Elegant Trogon, White-bellied Chacalaca and Sulphur-winged Parakeet. You may be lucky and see a Sun Bittern, which inhabits the forest streams. Butterflies, such as the Blue Morpho and Owl Butterfly, are common. Beware of snakes – Boa Constrictors have been reported.

Visitors to Cabo Blanco are limited to 40 a day. Book in advance and report to the Ranger Station, which is open Wed–Sun 08:00–16:00. After a short talk, visitors are allowed to use the single trail that runs for 5km (3 miles) down through the forest to the beach.

Getting There

Take the Pan-American Highway from San José to Puntarenas, a ferry to the peninsula, then a bus to Montezuma. Shuttle bus go several times a day from Montezuma to the park entrance.

Cabo Blanco Absolute Nature Reserve

Location: At the extreme south of the Nicoya Peninsula, 11km (7 miles) from Montezuma backpacker resort.
Size: 1175ha (2903 acres).
Altitude: Sea level to 150m (492ft).
Climate: Hot, humid and rainy in the wet season, very hot from Dec–Apr.
Of Interest: Tropical moist forest; sea birds.

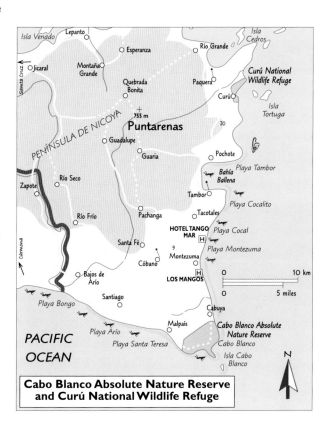

Cabo Blanco Absolute Nature Reserve and Curú National Wildlife Refuge

South Nicoya/Tempisque Conservation Area

Curú National Wildlife Refuge

Location: 8km (5 miles) south of Paquera on the coast of the south Nicoya Peninsula.

Size: 84ha (207 acres).

Altitude: Sea level to 20m (66ft).

Climate: Hot in the dry season, humid and rainy in the wet season.

Of Interest: Dry tropical forest, mangroves, turtle-nesting beach, migrating whales offshore.

Accommodation

No lodgings in the park itself, but possibilities in nearby Montezuma to suit all pockets:

Hotel Los Mangoes, on the road to Cabo Blanco, Montezuma, tel: 2642 0076, www.hotellosmangoes.com Highly recommended hotel with 10 rooms and 9 thatched bungalows, with all facilities. Landscaped gardens with waterfall and Jacuzzi.

Hotel Amor de Mar, on a headland just past the river, Montezuma, tel: 2642 0262, www.amordemar.com Well-run, American-owned hotel in pleasant grounds with hammocks under the trees; there are 14 comfortable rooms at varying prices.

Curú National Wildlife Refuge

Based on a working hacienda, this small reserve of 84ha (207 acres) has a variety of life zones, including primary dry forest, mangroves and a beautiful white sand beach on which Hawksbill and Olive Ridley turtles nest. The largest beach is excellent for swimming and offers good snorkelling possibilities. Humpback whales are often seen offshore in the nearby Bahia Ballena or Whale Bay (January is the best month), while mangroves extend along the small River Curú. There is a wide range of birds and mammals for such a small area. Guided walks are led by the resident scientists and you are bound to see Capuchin, Spider and Howler monkeys, Agoutis, Variegated Squirrels, White-tailed Deer and Armadillos, while massive iguanas hang around the refuge station. The birds are typical of the dry tropical forest and include Black-headed Trogons, Turquoise-browed Motmots, Rose-throated Becards, Lesser Ground Cuckoos, Hoffman's Woodpecker and Green-backed Heron, while offshore, Royal Terns, Magnificent Frigatebirds and Brown Pelicans maintain a regular patrol. The entrance to the reserve is 8km (5 miles) south of the village of Paquera. Advance booking is essential – tel: 2661 2392.

There are other possibilities in the area. Nearby is the beautiful uninhabited Isla Tortuga (Turtle Island), a popular day destination from San José and Puntarenas. The island has sandy beaches, backed by palm trees and other lush vegetation, while barbecues smoke away and marimba bands are usually in attendance. The snorkelling is excellent and a wide range of fish and crustaceans

Curú National Wildlife Refuge

can be spotted. Fishermen from the small fishing village of Tambor in Bahia Ballena run sunset bird-watching cruises through the mangroves of the Pachote Creek.

Getting There

Take the Pan-American Highway from San José to Puntarenas, a ferry to Pacquera, then the local bus.

Accommodation

A small amount of basic accommodation may be available at the reserve, but this is normally reserved for scientists and students. There are plenty of hotel rooms and bungalows at the nearby Tambor development. Also:

Hotel Tango Mar, Playa Tambor, tel: 2683 0001, www.tangomar.com This luxury eco-hotel is set among palms behind a deserted white sand, turtle-nesting beach. Exemplary food and service, plus nine-hole golf course.

Laughing Gulls

Passengers on the Puntarenas to Paquera ferry are often fascinated by the scores of Laughing Gulls (*Larus atricilla*) that accompany the ferry, not just in its wake, but alongside the decks, scavenging for food, which they will actually take from the hand. Laughing Gulls are the most common gull to be found on both the Caribbean and Pacific coasts of Costa Rica, only likely to be confused with the smaller Franklin's Gull. Laughing Gulls are renowned scavengers and are particularly common in the harbours of Puerto Limón and Puntarenas, where they feed on offal and scraps from fishing boats. They are omnivorous and will chase small crabs on mud flats and try to rob pelicans before they have a chance to swallow their prey, as well as begging for food from picnickers and holiday-makers on beaches.

The adult Laughing Gull is a handsome bird with a black head and a longish red bull. The back is slaty grey and the underparts white, with black wingtips and dark legs. It is buoyant in flight, but rarely glides. Its call is a high pitched 'ha…ha…ha' – hence the name. Laughing Gulls are largely found in Costa Rican waters in the winter, when the majority of the birds are immature.

Tambor – a Glimpse of the Future?

Tambor, the biggest resort development in Costa Rica (although it will eventually be surpassed by the Papagayo Project), has been dogged by controversy from the start. The Spanish developers have been accused of breaching several environmental laws, including destroying mangroves, taking beach sand and river gravel, building on the first 50m (165ft) of beach (which should be public property), and ignoring health and safety regulations. Despite court orders and public outcry, the project has gone ahead and is now almost complete. Nevertheless, the visitor may well be pleasantly surprised, because it has to be said that the development can scarcely be seen, either from the road or from the sea, and has little visual impact on the area.

CENTRAL PACIFIC CONSERVATION AREA

The area stretches south from Puntarenas and contains considerable contrasts in scenery, climate, vegetation and population. It is administered from the once-prosperous port of Puntarenas. In the 1800s, convoys of ox carts would bring coffee beans here for export via Cape Horn to Europe – a long and hazardous route. The building of the 'jungle train' from San José to the Caribbean port of Limón sounded the death knell for Puntarenas. Another blow has been the construction of the nearby deep-water port of Caldera, which can take container ships and cruise liners. Today, Puntarenas has the faded, neglected look of many tropical ports, but it remains a busy fishing port, while ferryboats ply the routes to the southern part of the Nicoya Peninsula. The name Puntarenas means 'sandy point', and the town is built on a narrow sandy spit with a mangrove estuary to the north and the Pacific to the south. Bird-watchers can see Laughing Gulls, Magnificent Frigatebirds, Brown Pelicans and Egrets on the estuary. A little to the south is the coastal town of Jacó, popular with *josefinos* at the weekends as it is the nearest holiday resort to the capital. The landscape changes further south; around Quepos, the moist forest has been cleared for plantations of oil palms. Eventually the popular Manuel Antonio National Park is reached. Although it is the smallest of Costa Rica's national parks, it attracts more visitors than any other.

Central Pacific Top Ten

Magnificent Frigatebird

Brown Pelican

Scarlet Macaws

Crocodiles

Poison Dart Frogs

Anteaters

Humpback Whales

All four species of monkey, including Squirrel Monkey

Boat-billed Heron

Green Marine Iguanas

Opposite, top to bottom:
Cathedral Point and one of several pristine beaches in the Manuel Antonio National Park; the Bananaquit is a common bird of the wet lowlands; Marine Iguanas can be found in parts of the southern Pacific coast, where they graze on algae in saltwater pools.

Central Pacific Conservation Area

Peñas Blancas Wildlife Refuge

Some 33km (20 miles) northeast of Puntarenas is the little-known reserve of Peñas Blancas. It covers 2400ha (5930 acres) of forest where rivers drain off the Cordillera de Tilarán. It is named after white cliffs of diatomaceous material found there – and indeed the reserve may be of more interest to geologists than ecologists, as there has been much forest clearance and only around 70 species of birds have been recorded here. Howler and Capuchin Monkeys, however, can be seen and also Red Brocket Deer. There are a few trails and camping is permitted, but there are no visitor facilities, so it is hardly surprising that Peñas Blancas is rarely high on an ecotourist's visiting list.

Carara National Park

In contrast to the above, Carara is well worth a visit. In fact, in terms of visitor numbers it is one of the most popular reserves in the country. There are a number of reasons for this. The first is accessibility – Carara is a mere two hours from San José and right on the main road leading to the coast. Secondly, Carara has a vast range of wildlife because it occupies a transition zone between tropical moist forest and tropical wet forest and has species from both habitats. The trees, therefore, are a mixture of evergreen and deciduous varieties. The park also includes stretches of the Tárcoles River, with its marshy flood plain and a particularly attractive oxbow lake covered with water hyacinths.

Before entering the reserve, take some time to stop at the nearby Tárcoles River Bridge, which is possibly the best place in the country to observe crocodiles. Scores of these fearsome reptiles can be seen lounging on the tidal mud, accompanied by vultures scavenging for any food scraps left behind by the crocs.

The American Crocodile

There are two members of the crocodilian family in Costa Rica – the American Crocodile and the Caiman. The latter is common, but the American Crocodile (*Crocodylus acutus*) is considered endangered, due to pollution, hunting and loss of habitat. American Crocodiles inhabit areas where fresh and salt waters mix, such as tidal rivers and mangrove swamps. They have a scaly hide and in the wild can reach 4m (13ft) in length. The eyes,

Carara National Park

Location: Puntarenas Province, 90km (56 miles) from San José. Nearest town is Jacó.

Size: 4500ha (1112 acres).

Altitude: 10m (32ft) to 150m (492ft).

Climate: Hot and humid even in the dry season, which lasts from January to April. At the height of the rainy season, parts of the reserve may be under water.

Of Interest: Transition zone between the moist and wet tropical forest; river and flood plain. Best location for Scarlet Macaws in the country.

nostrils and ears are located on the top of the head, so that it can remain concealed in the water. They are distinguished from their cousin, the Alligator, by having a longer, thinner snout and teeth that show even when the mouth is closed. American Crocodiles normally slide along on their belly, but can use their legs and, indeed, can reveal a surprising turn of speed. They can be dangerous to humans – there have been cases in Costa Rica of children being killed by crocodiles – but their usual diet consists of fish, turtles and small mammals. American Crocodiles lay their eggs in sandy soil, the sex of the young being determined by the temperature of the ground around the eggs. Hatchlings are eaten by a number of predators, including herons, egrets, Anhingas and Raccoons.

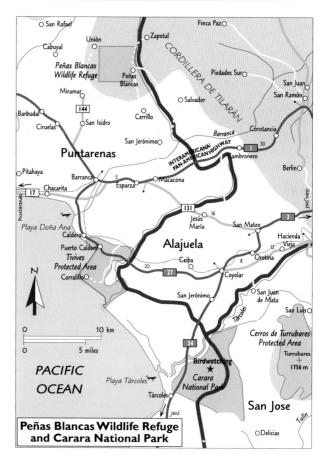

Peñas Blancas Wildlife Refuge and Carara National Park

Carara covers a mere 4500ha (1112 acres) but has a surprising number of mammal species, including Anteaters, Agoutis, Capuchin Monkeys and Coatis, while small cats such as Margay, Jaguarundi and Ocelot are occasionally seen. Carara is also a stronghold of a number of Costa Rica's seven species of poison dart frogs and it has also recorded 19 out of Costa Rica's 22 poisonous snakes. It is the birds, however, that most people come to see – particularly the Scarlet Macaw, which breeds in the park. Other attractions include various toucans, trogons and guans, while along the riverside stretch a variety of egrets and herons can be spotted including the strange Boat-billed Heron. The park is open daily 08:00–16:00. The ranger station is at the side of

Central Pacific Conservation Area

Carara was once part of a huge cattle ranch known as El Coyolar, with so much land that large areas of forest were never felled. The ranch was taken over by the Costa Rican Land Reform Agency in the 1970s and divided into small farms for landless peasants, but fortunately the Agency had the foresight to pass the forested area on to the National Parks Service. A biological reserve was set up, which initially had few visitors, but with the growth of tourism and the designation of Carara as a national park, numbers have grown and it is now one of the five most visited sites in the national parks system.

the Coastal Highway 3km (1.8 miles) south of the bridge. The trails start from here. Guides are available and highly recommended.

Scarlet Macaws

The jewel in the crown of Carara is the Scarlet Macaw (*Ara macao*). This unmistakable bird is notable for its gaudy colouring and long pointed tail and wings. Adults are mostly bright red, and have blue wings with a large yellow patch on each wing covert. The powerful bill is ivory-coloured. Scarlet Macaws feed in the canopy of evergreen or deciduous forests on nuts and fruit, often in family groups. They are noisy in flight, with strong, shallow wing beats. They nest during the dry season in cavities in trees and sometimes enlarge woodpecker holes. There are around 150 Scarlet Macaws nesting and breeding at Carara. A spectacular sight occurs at dusk, when they fly west down the River Tárcoles to roost in the coastal mangroves.

Right: *Large, colourful and raucous, the Scarlet Macaw is easy to identify. The Carara National Park is the best place to see them.*

Manuel Antonio National Park

Getting There

From San José take the Pan-American Highway west to the
Atenas exit. Follow the old highway to Orotina. Take the Jacó
turnoff and follow the coastal highway to the bridge over the
Tárcoles River. The ranger station is 3km (1.8 miles) to the south.

Accommodation

There is no accommodation in the park, but plenty of hotels and
lodges in nearby Playa Tárcoles and Jacó.

Tarcol Lodge, Playa Tárcoles, tel: 2430 0400,
www.costaricagateway.com Rustic lodge with comfortable
rooms and restaurant serving fresh seafood. Resident bird guide.
Villa Caletas, Tárcoles, tel: 2637 0606,
www.distinctivehotels.com Luxury establishment with a
stunning clifftop location surrounded by rainforest. Most
rooms have ocean views. Outstanding restaurant.
Copacabana, north central Jacó, tel: 2643 1005,
www.copacabanahotel.com Comfortable Canadian-owned
hotel with pool and sports bar. On the beach.

Manuel Antonio National Park

With a mere 682ha (1685 acres) of land, Manuel Antonio is one
of the smallest of Costa Rica's national parks, but because of its
stunning beaches, beautiful trails through the lush rainforest, easy
accessibility and a superb range of wildlife, it is one of the
country's most visited parks (probably competing with Poás for
the top position). There are four idyllic beaches – Espadilla Sur,
Manuel Antonio, Escondido and Playita – scimitars of white sand
backed by swaying palms and rainforest teeming with wildlife.
Central to the park is a headland at the end of which is Cathedral
Point. This was once an island, but it is now joined to the
mainland by a sand spit (known to geographers as a tombolo).
This is covered with water at high tide. To enter the reserve it
may be necessary to wade through this water. At low tide it is no
problem and easy to negotiate, but at high tide it can be a metre
and a half deep. Check with the rangers about the state of the
tide. A path (the most popular trail in the park) then leads to
Cathedral Point at 72m (236ft), with various viewing points en
route giving superb views of the offshore islands. The path then

**Manuel Antonio
National Park**

Location: Pacific coast, 7km (4 miles)
south of Quepos.
Size: 682ha (1685 acres).
Altitude: Sea level to 50m (160ft).
Climate: Hot, wet and humid – some
rain can be expected even in the dry
season. Rainfall total is 3000mm
(151in). January and February are the
driest months.
Of interest: Tropical lowland
rainforest, beaches and offshore
islands. For information, visit
www.manuelantoniopark.com

Central Pacific Conservation Area

The creation of Manuel Antonio National Park was a triumph for local conservation. The area had for a long time been in private hands although the public had always been allowed to use the beaches. Then, in 1968, the land was bought by an American, who put up fences and gates to keep the public out. After vandalism by locals, the local council ruled that the road must remain open and access to the beach should not be restricted. The land was then bought by a Frenchman, who planned to develop the land as a resort. At this stage, in 1972, the area was expropriated by the government and declared a national park, with additional land added in 1980. Ironically, the NPS still blocks the road with a gate!

returns to the mainland beaches, which are wonderful for picnics and swimming – although beware of Capuchin Monkeys, who will steal food and anything else that they can get their hands on.

There are interesting trees in the park, such as the shoreside manchineel or 'beach apple' – it is highly toxic, so don't eat the apple-like fruit. The park has stands of mangroves, with red, white and buttonwood varieties. Offshore a number of small islands provide nesting sites for sea birds, including the Brown Pelican, Anhinga and the Magnificent Frigatebird. In the inland forest, rich in wildlife, all four species of monkey – Howler, Spider, Capuchin and Squirrel – can be seen.

Squirrel Monkeys

The rarest of Costa Rica's four monkey species is the Squirrel Monkey (*Saimiri oerstedii*). Costa Rica is the most northerly country in its distribution and here it must be considered endangered, because of loss of habitat and poaching. There are probably less than 2000 animals in the wild. It is only found in Manuel Antonio National Park and further south in the Osa Peninsula, although there is a healthy population in neighbouring Panama and in the northern countries of South America.

Squirrel Monkeys have short-cropped fur which varies in colour from olive to yellowish orange. The mouth is black and the ears and eye surrounds are white. They are the smallest of the Costa Rican monkeys, growing up to 35cm (13.7in) plus a tail of 42cm (16.5in). The tail is not prehensile, but is used to balance when jumping through the trees. Squirrel Monkeys live in groups or troops of up to 20 and spend most of their daylight time in the canopy or middle levels of the forest, actively foraging for insects and fruits (they are not leaf-eaters). Females give birth to a single baby timed to coincide with the wet season and the youngster is carried on the mother's back from day one. It will be independent of the mother after about nine months. The main predators of Squirrel Monkeys are eagles and porcupines, but their appealing nature has meant that they are a prime target for poachers. At Manuel Antonio, troops of Squirrel Monkeys have been known to scavenge in the grounds of hotels and can be readily attracted if food is provided.

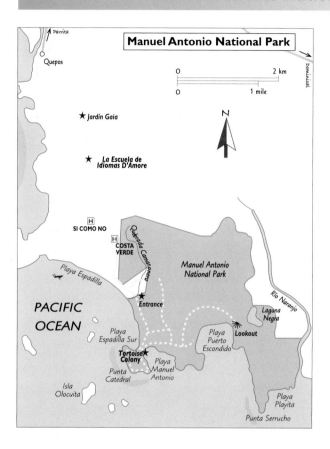

Other mammals often seen in Manuel Antonio are Three-toed
Sloths (which are attracted to the cecropia trees), Coatis,
Raccoons, Marmosets, Ocelots and River Otters. Over 350
species of birds have been recorded, such as the Green Kingfisher,
Laughing Falcon, Lineated and Red-crowned Woodpeckers,
Blue-crowned Motmot, Rufous-tailed Hummingbird, various
tanagers, Bananaquit and Red-legged Honeycreeper.

The popularity of Manuel Antonio has brought its own difficulties.
With over 150,000 visitors a year comes the problem of overuse.
At one stage the park authorities considered closing the park
completely for a spell to let it recover from the pounding of many
feet. Eventually it was decided to close the park on Mondays and

Central Pacific Conservation Area

limit the numbers to 600 a day. It is essential, therefore, to arrive early, before the quota has been reached. Manuel Antonio is open 07:00–16:00 and guides can be hired.

Getting There
It is four hours' drive from San José, taking the Pan-American Highway. Take the Jacó turn-off and follow the coastal highway to Quepos and a further 7km (4.4 miles) to Manuel Antonio. Daily SANSA flights go from San José to Quepos.

Accommodation
There is no accommodation within the park and no camping is allowed. There are, however, a number of hotels in the vicinity to suit all pockets:

Hotel Costa Verde, Manuel Antonio, Apdo. 89 Escazú, tel: 2777 0584, www.hotelcostaverde.com Apartments and villas

Right: A bird of marshlands and mudflats, the White Ibis is particularly common in the Caño Negro region and the Gulf of Nicoya.

Marino Ballena National Park

with balconies and sea views. Nature trails. Open-sided restaurant with views of sloths and Squirrel Monkeys.
Hotel Si Como No, Manuel Antonio, tel: 2777 0777, www.sicomono.com Si Como No (meaning 'yes, why not?') is an extraordinary, eco-friendly, award-winning hotel, with amazing architecture and decoration. Ocean views from all rooms.
Hotel California, Apdo 159 Quepos, tel: 2777 1234. French-run, three-storey hotel. Rooms have queen-sized beds, with verandas and ocean views.
Vista Serena, Manuel Antonio, tel: 2777 5162, www.vista serena.com One of the few good-value budget options at Manuel Antonio; 12 simple, but comfortable rooms with balconies. Small restaurant and kitchen for guests to use.

Marino Ballena National Park

This park was created in 1990 to protect the area's coastal waters. It covers 5161ha (12,752 acres) of ocean along with 172ha (425 acres) of coastline. The park includes Punta Uvita, where a sandy spit connects with an island forming a tombolo and two offshore islands, Las Tres Hermanas and Isla Ballena, that provide nesting sites for Magnificent Frigatebirds, Brown Boobies, Brown Pelicans and White Ibis. The underwater area is the site of the largest coral reef on the Pacific coast of Costa Rica. Environmentalists, however, are worried by the effect the construction of the coastal highway has had on the coral reef. The movement of earth and the felling of trees has polluted the water and the latest estimate is that 60% of the coral has been destroyed. Shrimp trawling is also a threat. The tiny village of Bahia is the location of a turtle-nesting beach – Hawksbill and Olive Ridley turtles come ashore between May and November – with a protection arrangement administered by the local community. Also of interest are the Green Marine Iguanas that graze on the algae in the saltwater pools. The name *ballena* means 'whale' and Humpback and Pilot Whales are frequently seen offshore. It used to be thought that the Humpbacks were on migration to their breeding grounds off Mexico and Hawaii, but improved identification techniques suggest that some of the whales may breed in Costa Rican waters. In addition to the whales, dolphins are abundant, and Common and Bottlenose Dolphins are seen throughout the year.

OSA CONSERVATION AREA

The Osa Peninsula boasts one of the largest remaining areas of coastal rainforest in Central America, stretching for 60km (37 miles) between the Pacific Ocean and Golfo Dulce. The whole peninsula has a frontier atmosphere about it, with redundant banana workers attempting to establish smallholdings or trying their luck at panning for gold. The area has been discovered as a tourist venue in recent years and despite its remoteness, it is popular with young backpackers for hikes and forest trekking, while more affluent visitors stay at the recently opened wildlife and sport-fishing lodges. Much of the peninsula is taken up by the remote and beautiful Corcovado National Park, while lying offshore is the Isla del Caño Biological Reserve, which has some marvellous coral reefs. To the east of Golfo Dulce is a narrow coastal plain, mainly taken up with bananas and oil palms. The chief town here is Golfito, which was built by the United Fruit Company for its workers. When the company pulled out in 1985, decline set in, but now tourism is slowly taking off and the government has given the town a further boost by making it a duty-free port. There are two other reserves on this side of the gulf. The Piedras Blancas National Park was originally set up with help from the Austrian government. Close to the town of Golfito is the Golfito National Wildlife Refuge, which was designated with the aim of protecting the settlement's watershed.

Osa Peninsula Top Ten

Scarlet Macaw
Monkeys, including the
    Squirrel Monkey
Tapir
Jaguar
Margay
Agouti
King Vulture
Coati
Peccaries
Frogs
Sea Turtles

Opposite, top to bottom:
The Margay, one of the smaller wild cats found in the Costa Rican forests; the Howler Monkey's call is said to be the loudest in the animal world; the spectacular Lobster-claw Heliconia is a common feature in botanical gardens and parks.

Osa Conservation Area

Isla del Caño Biological Reserve

Lying some 20km (12 miles) west of the Osa Peninsula and covering around 300ha (741 acres), Caño Island is noted mainly for its coral reef. The water is warm and snorkellers and divers can see abundant marine life including Spiny Lobsters, Sea Urchins, Sea Cucumbers, Manta Rays, Moray Eels, Sea Snakes, Barracuda and a whole range of colourful tropical fish. Beneath the low cliffs, the white sand beaches are attractive to Olive Ridley Turtles, while the offshore waters contain migrating Humpback and Pilot Whales and plenty of Common and Bottlenose Dolphins. The island has only 13 species of terrestrial birds, but plenty of sea birds, such as the Brown Booby. There is a variety of interesting land animals, such as the Boa Constrictor, the introduced Paca and Opossums.

Caño's other claim to fame is of an archaeological nature, as it was a pre-Columbian burial ground. The famous lithic spheres of the Diquis tribe (see panel, page 106) are found here in abundance, along with other artefacts.

Many of the lodges on the mainland run tours to the island. There is a single trail that runs inland from the ranger station through the forest. Camping is allowed on the beach near the ranger station, but there are no facilities.

Corcovado National Park

Of all the national parks and other protected areas in Costa Rica, Corcovado is undoubtedly the most remote and beautiful. At around 42,000ha (104,000 acres), Corcovado has wide biological diversity due to its remoteness and the fact that it has suffered little disturbance by humans in the past. The hot, wet climate – rainfall averages 4000mm (158in) – promotes eight habitats including mangrove swamps, montane forest, lowland rainforest, and Jollito palm groves. Corcovado also has sandy beaches, freshwater lakes and tidal estuaries. The forest areas are spectacular, with some of the tallest trees reaching 50m (165ft) and sporting enormous buttresses, which help to support the tree in the thin tropical soil. The trees are swathed with lianas and epiphytes, while there is a luxuriant shrub growth at lower levels. Biologists report over 100 different types of tree within one square hectare. Such a biomass

---

**Corcovado
National Park**

Location: Southern Costa Rica, Puntarenas Province, southern part of the Osa Peninsula.
Size: 42,000ha (104,000 acres).
Altitude: Sea level to 745m (2444ft) at Cerros Rincón.
Climate: Hot and wet throughout the year, with a drier period January to April. September and October are the wettest months.
Of Interest: Variety of habitats, including lowland rainforest, cloud forest, Jollito palm forest, mangrove swamps and coastal habitats, all teeming with wildlife, including many endangered species.

Corcovado National Park

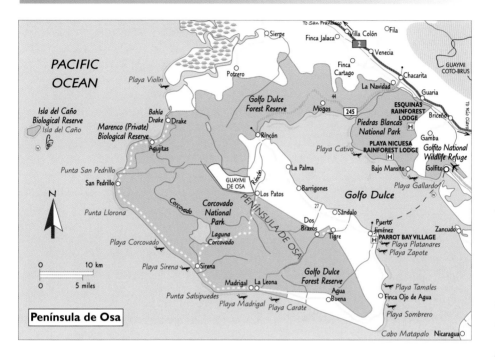

Península de Osa

supports an incredible range of wildlife. Just consider these statistics: there are over 400 species of birds, including 20 endemics; 139 types of mammals have been recorded (which is 10% of all the mammals in the Americas); over 100 types of amphibians and reptiles can be seen, including 42 species of frog and 28 species of lizard; there may be as many as 10,000 types of insects in Corvovado, amongst which are 28 species of butterfly.

What to Look Out For in Corcovado

All four of Costa Rica's monkey species – Howler, Capuchin, Spider and the endangered Squirrel – can be seen here. The Squirrel Monkey's only other home is at Manuel Antonio. The country's six wild felines also live at Corcovado. You will be lucky to see the Jaguar, although its distinctive paw marks are often spotted on the muddy trails. There is more chance of seeing the Margay, which is about the size of a domestic cat and likes to sun itself on rocks. The Ocelot is extremely shy and well camouflaged. The other felines are the small, dark-coloured Jaguarundi, the Puma

Osa Conservation Area

The Diquis

Of all the *indigenas* groups of pre-Columbian Costa Rica, the Diquis are perhaps the most remarkable. From their homeland in the northern part of the Osa Peninsula, they fashioned the gold jewellery that so excited Columbus. It is highly likely that they were also responsible for the lithic spheres – perfect stone balls – found throughout the southwest of the country. How they were able to make these large granite spheres and take them to the Isla del Caño, some 20km (12 miles) offshore, still excites debate.

or mountain lion, which is almost as large as the Jaguar, and the tiny Oncilla. Other mammals that could be seen include the shy Baird's Tapir, a large animal with a vaguely horse-like head and a hanging upper lip or proboscis. Bands of aggressive Peccaries are common, as are Agoutis, which forage in the undergrowth, and Coatis, a member of the raccoon family with long ringed tails. There is also a good chance of seeing the River Otter, anteaters, sloths and crab-eating raccoons. The beaches of Corcovado provide nesting sites for all four of Costa Rica's sea turtles – the Hawksbill, Olive Ridley, Green and Leatherback. Amongst the birds are around 1200 Scarlet Macaws. Although their population is relatively healthy, the macaws still suffer badly from poaching. The estuaries and Lake Corcovado provide a fruitful habitat for a variety of egrets and herons, including the strange Boat-billed Heron. The rarest of Costa Rica's vultures, the King Vulture, is also found here. The huge Harpy Eagle, which preys on arboreal mammals such as sloths and monkeys, is now nearly extinct in Costa Rica, but a few pairs may remain in Corcovado. The park is also a great area for hummingbirds, supporting around 16 species. Reptiles and amphibians include crocodiles, which lurk around the estuaries, 40 species of frog (such as Red eyed, Rain, Glass and Poison Arrow

Right: The Strawberry Poison Dart Frog, sometimes known as the Blue Jeans Frog. There is no evidence, incidentally, that indigenous groups in Costa Rica used the frogs' poisonous skin secretions in hunting.

Corcovado National Park

Frogs) and scores of snakes – amongst their number are the dangerous Boa Constrictors and Bushmaster. There are over 10,000 species of insects, many unwelcome to humans, and 100 plus butterflies. Finally, mention must be made of the 50 species of bats, including fruit- and fish-eating varieties.

Walking Corcovado's Trails

Corcovado has three entry points: San Pedrillo at the northwest corner; La Leona in the southeast, and Los Patos on the northern edge of the park. All have ranger stations. In addition, the park headquarters and research station is at Sirena in the centre of the reserve. There is also a remote ranger station at Los Planes in the north. All of these have short trails and are linked with each other by longer hiking trails, some following beaches for long stretches. The lengthier hikes require considerable rainforest trekking experience, with wet-weather equipment essential. Hikers should be aware of some of the difficulties: the paths can be extremely muddy, especially in the wet season; insects such as mosquitoes and horseflies can be a major irritation; some trails involve fording tidal rivers – beware of crocodiles and strong tows; the beach trails may mean crossing rocky headlands, with the possibility of being cut off by high tides, so purchase a tide table before setting off; sharks have been known to come up the estuaries at high water; some hikers have been threatened by groups of aggressive peccaries. However, don't be put off – scores of backpackers trek through the Corcovado trails daily without incident.

The Park Administration Office is in Puerto Jimenez, next to the Banco Nacional. It is open Mon–Fri 07:30–12:00 and 13:00–17:00, tel: 2735 5036. There is an entry fee to the park, which can be halved with advance purchase.

Pigs of the Forest

Few forest mammals, even members of the cat family, are dangerous to walkers. An exception is the Peccary. There are two varieties in Costa Rica, the Collared Peccary (*Tayassu tajacu*) and the White-lipped Peccary (*Tayassu pecari*). Collared Peccaries are the more abundant of the two, appearing a in a variety of habitats, and are distinguished by a band of lighter coloured hair around

Gold in the Park

Columbus was impressed with the gold ornaments worn by the native Indians in Costa Rica, and much of this valuable mineral was panned from the streams on the Osa Peninsula. The gold industry revived in the 1980s and many of the gold miners or *oreros* were banana workers made redundant when United Fruit closed down in 1985. When the Corcovado National Park was set up, there were over 3000 *oreros* working within the park's boundaries, causing considerable damage through mining river beds, polluting rivers and felling trees. They were evicted and promised compensation. This was slow to arrive and protests ensued, the *oreros* camping out in parks in San José. At the moment there is an uneasy truce, and panning for gold is still an activity that is often seen in the rivers of the Osa Peninsula.

Osa Conservation Area

the neck. White-lipped Peccaries are slightly larger, having a white patch of hair on the chin and being confined to rainforest areas.

These pig-like creatures have tusk-like canine teeth and root in the ground for vegetation, feeding on stems, bulbs, fruit and small vertebrates. They like to wallow in mud and shallow water.

Peccaries were hunted for food and hides for centuries before Europeans came to Costa Rica and this still goes on, although they are not considered endangered. Collared Peccaries forage around in small groups of up to 30, but White-lipped Peccaries can be seen in bands of over 100. Both species can be aggressive and noisy, clicking their teeth and grunting in an alarming fashion. Dominant males have even been known to charge at hikers in the forest. The general advice if attacked in this way is to climb the nearest tree, which could be difficult as many of the rainforest trunks have vicious spikes. The alternative move is to stand absolutely still and wait for the animals to get bored and go away – a strategy that requires a strong will!

Below: Trees in the primary forest of the Osa Peninsula, showing typical buttress roots.

Getting There

Take the Pan-American Highway from San José south to Piedras Blancas. Turn right for Puerto Jiménez. It is 395km (240 miles) by road. A quicker option is by air. There are daily flights from San José to Golfito, Puerto Jiménez and Drake Bay using SANSA and Travelair. Charter flights can be arranged directly to Sirena Biological Station.

Accommodation

Camping is allowed at the ranger stations at the edge of the park. There is also some modest bunkhouse accommodation at the ranger stations. Prior reservations are necessary. There is more comfortable accommodation available at Puerto Jiménez:

Parrot Bay Village, on the beach west of the dock, Puerto Jiménez, tel: 2735 5180, www.parrotbayvillage.com Wooden framed bungalows with all facilities. Open-air restaurant. Kayaks are available for guests to explore the mangroves.

La Choza del Manglare, Puerto Jiménez, tel: 2735 5002. Lodge with cabins. Riverside restaurant. Wildlife, including Capuchin Monkeys and Scarlet Macaws, can be seen in the grounds.

Piedras Blancas National Park

Once the Esquinas section of the Corcovado National Park, Piedras Blancas was made a national park in its own right in 1999. It was also once known as the 'Rainforest of the Austrians' (see History below). It also incorporates La Gamba Biological Station, which carries out ecological research. Piedras Blancas consists largely of primary evergreen rainforest, covering some 14,000ha (34,600 acres), with some extremely tall trees including the espave, the Silk Cotton and the Possum Wood, giants that can reach up to 70m (230ft) in height. Vegetation is prolific at other layers, too, with Heliconias and Royal Palms in the luxuriant undergrowth. Rivers, with numerous waterfalls, drain the forest and lead to stunning beaches. As might be expected, the wildlife, which is still being recorded, is outstanding. All of Costa Rica's monkey species – Howler, Spider, Capuchin and Squirrel – can be seen, while other mammals include the Coati, Raccoon, Agouti, Paca and anteaters. It is also one of the last remaining homes of the Jaguar in Costa Rica. Piedras Blancas is considered one of the best bird-watching spots in the country and is home to Scarlet Macaws, Chestnut-mandibled Toucans, White Hawks and a host of other rarities. A number of trails have been opened up, with guides available, but as yet there are few facilities.

The History of Piedras Blancas

In 1991, the Austrian classical violinist, Michael Schnitzler, founded the 'Rainforest of the Austrians', an organization formed to raise money to buy land in the Esquinas area to preserve the

Piedras Blancas National Park

Location: Close to the town of Golfito, on Golfo Dulce, Puntarenas province.
Size: 14,000ha (34,640 acres).
Altitude: Sea level to around 1000m (3280ft).
Climate: Hot and wet throughout the year, with 5076mm (200 in) of rain annually
Of Interest: Primary rainforest with specimen trees and a wide variety of birds and mammals, including all four species of monkeys.

Osa Conservation Area

When Minor Keith built the Jungle Railway from San José to the Caribbean coast, he financed the last stretch by planting bananas along the trackside. The fruit became a major export, employing Jamaican railway workers. Keith formed the United Fruit Company (the Yunai), which was to have a profound sociological influence. On the plus side, the Yunai took a paternal interest in its workers, providing houses, schools and hospitals, while its workers were relatively well paid. On the debit side, it employed anti-union practices and would desert an area if faced with trouble. After strikes in the 1930s it moved to the Pacific coast. The United Brands (as it is now known) then closed its banana operations in the Golfito area in 1985 when disease hit the crop, replacing them with the less labour-intensive oil palms and leaving many workers redundant. Many of the unemployed workers turned to prospecting for gold in the Osa Peninsula, while others have found work in tourism and ecology. The town of Golfito is slowly recovering, with the growth of tourism and its designation as a 'duty-free' port.

lowland rainforest. The Austrian government supported the enterprise and encouraged the organization to persuade local farmers to turn to ecotourism as an alternative source of income. The former farmers are now employed in running the park, the accommodation lodges and a botanical garden. The Rainforest of the Austrians also administers La Gamba Biological Station. Esquinas was incorporated in the Corcovado National Park in 1991. Eight years later, it became a national park with the name of Piedras Blancas.

Getting There
Take the Pan-American Highway south from San José to Palmar; 32km (20 miles) south of Palmar, take the turning to La Gamba and then follow the signs to Piedras Blancas National Park.

Accommodation
Esquinas Rainforest Lodge, Piedras Blancas National Park, Puntarenas Province, tel: 2775 0140, www.esquinaslodge.com Delightful lodge in the jungle, with a range of wildlife to be seen from the open-sided restaurant and cabin balconies; 220 species of birds counted in the grounds. Pool. Excursions organized.
Playa Nicuesa Rainforest Lodge, Piedras Blancas National Park, tel: 2735 5237, http://playanicuesa.com A beachside eco-lodge surrounded by rainforest. Guesthouse and cabins. Good restaurant serving local organic food. Kayaks for hire.

Jaguars
The Jaguar (*Panthera onca*) is the largest of Costa Rica's wild cats and the only New World example of the Panthera genus (the other three are the Old World tiger, lion and leopard). Its range extends from Mexico through Central America south to northern Argentina. It ranges across a variety of forested and open terrain, but in Costa Rica its preferred habitat is dense rainforest. The Jaguar is also notable in that it enjoys swimming and will often be found near to rainforest streams. The male Jaguars are large animals weighing 56–96kg (124–212lb) and measuring 1.62–1.83m (5–6ft), with females 10–20% smaller. The Jaguar (*El Tigre* in Costa Rica) is a largely solitary animal and catches its prey by stalking and ambushing. Biologists consider that it plays an important role in stabilizing ecosystems and regulating the populations of prey

Piedras Blancas National Park

species. The Jaguar has a powerful bite and its usual method of killing is to bite directly through the skull of its prey, delivering a fatal blow to the brain. It can even crack the shell of a turtle. The Jaguar prefers large prey and will catch deer, tapirs, peccary, monkeys and even caiman. Females generally prefer smaller prey. The coat of the Jaguar is usually tawny yellow, with rosettes or spots for camouflage in its jungle environment, but black melanistic forms have been noted – these are often called 'black panthers'. The Jaguar has often been described as nocturnal, but its main activity is around dawn and dusk, so 'crepuscular' would be a more accurate definition. Jaguars rarely attack humans and will flee quickly if spotted, but the normal advice if you surprise a Jaguar in Costa Rica is not to run away (this may stimulate the animal to give chase) but to face the animal, wave your arms to appear large and make as much noise as possible. This is usually enough to make the animal back off. Jaguars have lost much of their natural habitat in Costa Rica, through deforestation, and must be considered endangered. The best chance of spotting a Jaguar is in the various parks and reserves around Corcovado and the Osa Peninsula.

Below: *The Jaguar is the largest of Costa Rica's felines and its favoured habitat is dense rainforest.*

Osa Conservation Area

Golfito National Wildlife Refuge

Golfito National Wildlife Refuge

Location: On the shore of Golfo Dulce, Puntarenas Province, southern Costa Rica.

Size: 1309ha (3234 acres).

Altitude: Sea level to 400m (1312ft).

Climate: Hot, humid and wet – 5076mm (200in) of rainfall annually. Average temperature 27°C (81°F).

Of Interest: Evergreen tropical rainforest, beaches and a small coral reef. Wide variety of flora and fauna.

This small reserve occupies the forested hills behind the town of Golfito. It was spared deforestation and the planting of oil palms and bananas because of its steep slopes. The government eventually protected the area in order to preserve Golfito's water supply. Covering 1309ha (3234 acres), the reserve consists largely of evergreen rainforest stimulated by the heavy rainfall, which can amount to 5076mm (200in) annually. It has one of the tallest canopies in Central America, with some trees (such as Purple Heart, Butternut and Silk Cotton) reaching 43m (140ft) in height. There are also some unusual trees here, such as the Caryodaphnopsis, which occurs nowhere else in the country, and a 'living fossil' cycad called zamia. The Golfito reserve is one of the most accessible in the country, most of the trails leading up from the town or the coast road. The downside of this is that it has suffered badly from hunting. For this reason, Golfito has fewer species to be seen than Corcovado, despite having similar conditions. Nevertheless a wide range of mammals can be seen. All four species of Costa Rican monkeys live here, plus Agouti, Coati, Raccoons, Collared Peccary, Paca and, of the smaller cats, Margay and Jaguarundi. Nearly 150 species of birds have been identified at Golfito, including Scarlet Macaws, Barn Owls, and a number of birds with limited distribution, such as Yellow-billed Cotinga, Orange-collared Mannikin, Golden-naped Woodpecker, Riverside Wren and Baird's Trogon. The refuge also covers part of Golfo Dulce, where ghost crabs can be seen along the beach and dolphins and whales in the migration season. There is also a small coral reef. There are no facilities at the refuge, but numerous trails can be followed.

Agouti

One of the most common mammals in the dry, moist and wet forest areas along the Pacific coast is the Agouti (*Dasyprocta puncata*), known in Costa Rica as the *Guatusa*. Agoutis belong to the order Rodentia and are amongst the larger of the rodents, growing up to 60cm (24in) in length and weighing 4kg (9lb). They are generally orange-brown in colour, with a white underside. They have short hair and a squirrel-like head. The rear legs are long and the front legs much shorter. When feeding, Agoutis sit on their hind legs and hold food between their front paws. They

Golfito National Wildlife Refuge

feed largely on fruit and will sometimes bury their food, helping with seed dispersal. Agoutis will often follow troops of monkeys to pick up fruit that they drop from trees. A pair will mate for life, but are generally seen singly. They breed in hollow tree trunks or burrows amongst tree roots. The majority of young are born to coincide with the period when fruit is most abundant. Agoutis are diurnal but become increasingly nocturnal in areas where they are intensively hunted – they are favourite game animals throughout their range. In Costa Rica, they have a number of natural predators, such as the larger snakes and some of the bigger forest cats. There are dense populations of Agouti in the relatively undisturbed parts of Costa Rica and they are not considered endangered – indeed, they have been known to live for as long as 20 years, which is unusual for a rodent.

Getting There

From San José, take the Pan-American Highway south towards Panama. At the town of Río Claro, take the turn-off to Golfito. The total distance is 342km (212 miles). There is a public bus connecting San José with Golfito. Daily flights with SANSA and Travelair go to Golfito.

Below: *The diurnal Agouti is the most common mammal in the forest lands of the Pacific coast.*

Accommodation

There is no accommodation within the refuge, apart from camping (with permission). There are a number of possibilities in Golfito:

Las Gaviotas, Apdo. 12 Golfito, tel: 2775 0971. An expensive option on the waterfront. Elegant *cabinas* and a good restaurant overlooking Golfo Dulce serving tasty seafood dishes.

Hotel del Cerro, opposite the United Fruit dock, tel: 2775 0006. Chinese-owned small hotel, which includes an old restored cinema. Open-air roof restaurant.

CENTRAL VOLCANIC CONSERVATION AREA

Although widely referred to as the Valle Central, this area is an undulating upland lying between 1000m (3300ft) and 3000m (9800ft) above sea level, surrounded by volcanic mountains. To the north and east is the Cordillera Central, with the active volcanoes Poás and Irazú, each in their own national park. To the south is the start of the Cordillera de Talamanca, while to the west is the lower lying Fila de Bustamente, before the land drops down to the Pacific coastal plain.

The capital city, San José, sprawls across the Central Valley, containing an estimated 337,000 *josefinos*, plus one and a half million people in Greater San José. The feel of inner San José is North American, with its filigree of power lines, neon signs, fast-food outlets and protected parking lots.

Central Volcanic Area Top Ten

Active Volcanoes
Volcano Junco
Baird's Tapir
Great Curassow
Violet Sabrewing
King Vulture
Bare-necked Umbrellabird
Orchids at Lankester Gardens
Red-tailed Hawks
Armadillo

Opposite, top to bottom:
The pea-green coloured crater lake of Volcán Irazú; this rather dingy looking Clay-coloured Robin is, in fact, Costa Rica's national bird; coffee plantations are found throughout the Central Valley — coffee is one of Costa Rica's chief exports.

Central Volcanic Conservation Area

San José

San José has several attractions. The Teatro Nacional should not be missed, while there are a number of good museums. Away from the inner city, there are *barrios* such as Otoya and Amón, which have examples of colonial architecture in leafy boulevards. Further afield there are attractive suburbs such as the university centre of San Pedro. Above all, San José makes a convenient accommodation centre for visiting surrounding national parks and other wildlife reserves.

Over 60% of Costa Rica's population lives in the Valle Central and this includes a number of foreigners, attracted partly by the favourable climate. The National Geographic Society once concluded that two towns in the area – La Garita and Atenas – 'had the best climate in the world'. The region is the location of three provincial capitals – Alajuela, Cartago and Heredia – plus a host of attractive smaller towns and villages.

The fertility of the area's volcanic soil ensures that agriculture is the main form of employment. In Alajuela, fruit such as mangoes and strawberries dominate. Further east, in Heredia and Cartago provinces, coffee is king. On the higher, wetter lands, herds of Holstein cattle provide the bulk of the country's milk and cheese.

Despite the density of population and the importance of agriculture, there is plenty for the ecotourist to appreciate in the Central Valley, with four national parks and many other protected areas, butterfly farms and gardens – all within easy reach of the capital. Indeed, it is quite possible to take a trip to either the Caribbean or Pacific coasts and return within the day.

Volcán Poás National Park

One of the most popular excursions in central Costa Rica, for tourists and *Ticos* alike, is the walk to the top of Poás Volcano. Surrounded by its own protective national park, Poás is one of the most accessible volcanoes in the world. A long, winding road leads to a car park and the visitors' centre, from where it is a gentle 400m (440yd) walk to a viewing platform right at the rim of the crater. Poás, which is 2704m (8000ft) high, last had a significant eruption in 1989, but brief gas emissions and minor

Volcán Poás National Park

Location: Alajuela province, 64km (40 miles) north of San José.
Size: 5600ha (13,800 acres).
Altitude: Up to 2708m (8900ft).
Climate: Temperature varies widely – on sunny days it can reach 21°C (70°F), but when the clouds come down it can be chilly, so take warm clothing. Average rainfall is 3553mm (140in).
Of Interest: Stunning volcanic features. Stunted cloud forest, with some endemic wildlife.
Getting there: From San José take the highway to Alejuela. From there take the road to Itiquis and Fraijanes, following the signs to the volcano.
Accommodation: None in the park and no camping allowed.

Volcán Poás National Park

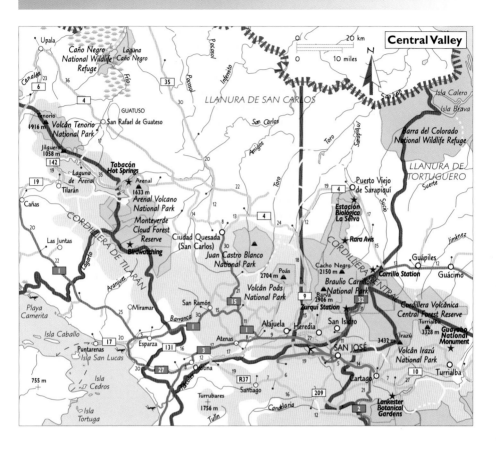

explosive activity can temporarily close the park to the public, as happened in 1994 and again in 2006, when the park was closed for 12 days. The crater, which is claimed to be one of the largest in the world, is about 1500m (1 mile) wide, 300m (984ft) deep and full of interest. During periods of volcanic calm there can be a bewitching turquoise-coloured lake, but after volcanic activity the water can disappear, being replaced by sulphurous gas and steam emissions, solfataras and even small geysers. A few metres back from the crater edge is the Botos Trail, running for 1.5km (0.9 mile) through dwarf forest, stunted by the cold, the ash and the acid rain emissions. The trail leads to an extinct side crater filled with rather acidic water containing little life. This is Botos Lake, named after a local *indigenas* tribe, long since disappeared from

Central Volcanic Conservation Area

Mario Boza

The story of conservation at Poás actually began in the Great Smoky Mountains National Park in Tennessee. A Costa Rican research student, Mario Boza, visited this park in the United States in the 1960s and was so impressed that on his return to Costa Rica he developed a plan to manage the area around Poás as a national park and presented this as his masters thesis. The plan was adopted and became the start of what was to be probably the most comprehensive system of national parks and refuges anywhere in the world.

the area. The viewing platform overlooking the lake is close to the highest point in the park and some visitors may suffer from breathlessness at this height. A further hike can be made along the Escalonia Trail, which runs for 1km (0.6 mile) through cloud forest. It is named after the escalonia tree, distinctive with its pagoda-like shape. This is the best place to see the park's two endemic species, the Poás Squirrel and the sparrow-like Volcano Junco. Other common birds include the Fiery-throated Hummingbird, Sooty-capped Bush-Tanager, Slaty Flowerpiercer, Mountain Eleania, Black-billed Nightingale-Thrush and the Black and Yellow Silky Flycatcher. Costa Rica's national bird, the Clay-coloured Robin, can also be seen in the Poás National Park.

The park has an attractive, modern visitors' centre (open 08:00–16:00) and a small museum, which describes the volcanic and ecological features of the area. There is a souvenir shop, a café serving drinks and snacks and an auditorium where audiovisual presentations are given on Sundays. It is best to visit Poás early in the morning, as by about 11:00 it is usually covered in cloud. Avoid weekends, if possible, as this is when *Ticos* come in their hundreds (tel: 2442 7041).

On the road up to Poás, on its eastern flanks and just outside the park boundary, is the frequently photographed and much visited Catarata La Paz (Peace Waterfall). Formerly known as the Angel Falls, the name was changed because of confusion with the better-known waterfalls in South America and to celebrate President Arias's peace efforts in Central America. The adventurous can walk behind the falling water, while the less brave can have some retail therapy at the numerous stalls selling craft ware at the side of the road.

Juan Castro Blanco National Park

The Clay-coloured Robin

It is curious that a country that has such exotic birds – such as the Resplendent Quetzel, Scarlet Macaws and numerous hummingbirds and parrots – should choose as its national bird a rather drab, brown species called the Clay-coloured Robin. A bird of suburban lawns and gardens, it does not even sing very often, confining its trilling to April. This month, however, is the start of the rainy season and the beginning of a fresh agricultural cycle, so the robin's song is a significant time marker.

Juan Castro Blanco National Park

Set up in 1992, Juan Castro Blanco is one of the least visited parks in the National Parks system. It was created to protect the primary rain- and cloud forest that forms the catchment area of a number of rivers such as the Toro, Platanar and Guayabo. There is a considerable amount of volcanic activity in the park. Volcán Platanar (2183m/7162ft) is still active, while others such as Volcán Porvenir (2267m/7438ft) and Volcán el Viejo (2122m/6962ft) are currently dormant. In addition there are numerous hot springs.

The rainforest area has three life zones and contains some magnificent trees, such as the Oak, Quizarra, White Cypress, Cedar, Magnolia and Yos. The trees are festooned with orchids and epiphytes, and the wildlife is predictably prolific. Nearly 60 species of mammal have been recorded in the park, including three of Costa Rica's four species of monkey, Baird's Tapir, Three-toed Sloth, Armadillo, Agouti, Coati, Red Brocket Deer and Paca. Felines are also present, particularly the Ocelot.

Amongst the birds, 233 species have been recorded, including colonies of Montezuma's Oropendula, Resplendent Quetzel, Three-wattled Bellbird, Bat Falcon, the rare Black Guan and Great Curassow. The park is also home to the Violet Sabrewing, the country's largest and most colourful hummingbird. Juan Castro Blanco also has 22 species of bats, 37 types of amphibians and reptiles (including the Boa Constrictor and the Fer-de-lance), 35 beetle species, 51 aquatic insects and 274 types of butterflies and moths. Clearly the park has great potential, but because the government has had difficulty in buying the land there are few facilities at present, except for a few rather rugged trails.

Juan Castro Blanco National Park

Location: Northwestern Central Valley, 100km (62 miles) north of San José, just to the east of Ciudad Quesada in Alajuela province.
Size: 14,258ha (35,231 acres).
Altitude: Between 700m (2296ft) and 2267m (7437ft).
Climate: Hot and wet, rainfall 3550mm (140in) a year.
Of Interest: Volcanic features, rainforest and cloud forest. Wide range of wildlife.

Opposite: Steam and gases rise from the main crater of Volcán Poás, Costa Rica's most accessible volcano.

Living Fences

Wherever there are cattle in Costa Rica, the pasture land is contained by 'living fences'. These are, in fact, the saplings of certain types of tree, spaced at regular distances, cut to a level height and joined by wire. Some of the trees are allowed to grow to their full height to provide shade for the cattle.

Central Volcanic Conservation Area

Butterfly Farms

Butterflies (*mariposas*) are abundant all over Costa Rica, where it is estimated that 10% of the world's species can be found. One national park claims to have recorded over 3000 species of butterflies and moths. A number of butterfly farms have been established in the country and pupae are now exported all over the world. Many of the farms are open to the public and there are some popular ones in the Central Valley, including **Spirogyra Jardin de Mariposas** in San José. Close to Alajuela is **La Guácima**, which claims to be the world's second largest exporter of butterflies (the largest is believed to be in Taiwan). Both farms have free-flying butterflies and guides to describe the complex butterfly life cycle. Morning visits are recommended, especially during the rainy season, as the butterflies tend to shelter when it is overcast.

Getting There
From San José take the road to Alajuela, then on to Ciudad Quesada (also known as San Carlos). The main entrance to the park is just to the east of the town.

Accommodation
There is no accommodation in the park, but plenty of possibilities in Ciudad Quesada:

El Tucano Resort, 8km (5 miles) northeast of Ciudad Quesada, tel: 2460 9091, www.occidental-hotels.com Luxury health resort with thermal waters, spa and jogging trail in the woods.

Hotel La Mirada, 4km (2.5 miles) north of Ciudad Quesada, tel: 2460 2222. Pleasant hotel located on a hill overlooking the central plains. Rooms with their own carport and private facilities.

Sloths
One of the oddest mammals in Costa Rica is the sloth, found countrywide. There are two types, the Brown-throated Three-toed Sloth (*Bradypus variegates*), which is active by day and night, and Hoffman's Two-toed Sloth (*Choloepus hoffmani*) which is largely nocturnal and unlikely to be seen by visitors. The former weighs around 4kg (9lb) and has a whitish face and brown body. The hair

Right: The Brown-throated Three-toed Sloth is the more common of the country's two sloth species, being active by day and night.

is long and stiff and often covered with greenish algae, which helps to camouflage them in the trees. Their relatively long legs end with feet that have three curved claws, which are used to hang upside down on the branches of trees. Sloths have a low metabolism and move extremely slowly. They descend from their tree once a week to defecate (a time when they are extremely vulnerable to predators, such as large snakes and cats.) Why they do this instead of defecating from up in the branches remains a mystery. However, the defecations fertilize the tree, which is then left to the sloth's single baby when it matures, the adult moving on to find another home. Sloths reach sexual maturity when they are three years old and may live for up to 20 years. They are kept clean by parasites, which lay eggs in the sloths' dung. It is known that a number of species of beetles and moths also spend at least part of their life cycles living on sloths.

Volcán Irazú National Park

A popular excursion near Cartago is the ascent to the summit of Volcán Irazú, with a spectacular drive through fields of coffee, potatoes and cabbages, replaced by dairy farms at higher levels. Set in its own national park, Irazú rises to 3432m (11,260ft), the highest of the volcanoes around the Central Valley. The summit has a complex of four craters, surrounded by swathes of dramatic volcanic ash. Diego de la Hoya crater (named after a Spanish governor, who first chronicled an eruption of Irazú in 1723) has a lake that is pea-green in colour, tinted by the minerals in the volcanic rock. A large adjacent crater is 300m (1080ft) deep. Another nearby crater is wide and shallow and covered with black volcanic ash, inviting comparisons with the surface of the moon. Irazú has erupted regularly over historical time, the last serious occasion being on 19 March 1963, the day when US President John F Kennedy visited the country. The eruption lasted for two years, sending up large columns of smoke and ash. On one occasion, ash-filled vapour was blown up into the clouds, leading to a storm that deposited several inches of mud over a wide area. Since then Irazú has been fairly quiet, apart from a minor eruption in 1994, when some fumerole activity occurred. The vegetation around the peak is predictably stunted, with blackened dwarf oaks, ferns and lichens. In such an environment, wildlife is obviously scarce, but two birds – the aptly named

National Hero

Visitors spending some time in the Central Valley town of Alajuela should search out the statue of **Juan Santamaría**, which is in the local park. Santamaría was a young drummer boy who distinguished himself in the fight against William Walker, the American filibuster, in the 19th century. At the battle at Rivas in Nicaragua, Santamaría volunteered to torch the fortress that Walker's men were defending. He succeeded and the battle was won, but he died in a hail of bullets. He is commemorated with a museum in his home town of Alajuela, while San José's international airport is named after him.

Volcán Irazú National Park

Location: Cartago province, 48km (30 miles) east of San José.
Size: 2309ha (5705 acres).
Altitude: Up to 3432m (11,260ft) at the summit.
Climate: Warm, with a pronounced dry season on the lower slopes. Cold and cloudy at the summit.
Of Interest: Volcanic features, with craters, crater lakes and fumeroles.

Central Volcanic Conservation Area

Above: The moon-like surface around the main crater of Volcán Irazú. Its last minor eruption was in 1994.

Volcano Junco and the Volcano Hummingbird – manage to survive. There is a ranger station 2km (1.25 miles) below the summit, a picnic site with tables, toilets and a mobile café, plus a small visitors' centre. Two trails lead from the car park to the summit. Good visibility is essential for a visit to Irazú, but don't be deterred by an apparent shroud of fog – the summit is often above the clouds and bathed in glorious sunshine. It is usually cold, however, with an average temperature on the summit of 7°C (45°F), so warm clothing is advisable. On a clear day the views can be staggering and it is sometimes possible to see both the Caribbean and Pacific coasts.

Accommodation
There is no accommodation within the park itself, but there are some good possibilities nearby, including:

Hacienda San Miguel Rancho Redondo, tel: 2229 5058. Comfortable lodge on a working dairy farm. Horse riding and guided hikes available.

Songbird Friendly Coffee
Coffee is now Costa Rica's most important export. A popular excursion from San José is to visit the *finca* of Café Britt, the country's biggest producer. The coffee tour begins with an audiovisual presentation describing the historical importance of coffee to Costa Rica, and this is followed by a tour of the plantation and the factory production processes. The visit is completed by coffee tasting. For such a big industry, it is inevitable that scientific advances have been made and these have not always been in the interest of the environment. In the early days of coffee growing, it was necessary to grow shade trees at intervals, but new strains of

Turrialba and Tenorio Volcano National Parks

coffee have been developed that make these unnecessary. This has had the effect of reducing the habitat available for North American songbirds, such as tanagers and flycatchers, which spend the winter in Costa Rica. Environmentalists campaigned for a return of the shade trees and it is now possible to buy 'songbird friendly' coffee. In another environmental development, an enterprising company in Costa Rica has come up with a brilliant idea that is typical of the country's ecological awareness. The firm obtains waste paper from neighbouring El Salvador and mixes it with actual brewed coffee and the skins of beans. The result takes the form of notepaper and writing pads, making a good souvenir for environmentally-minded visitors.

Volcán Turrialba National Park

This 1257ha (4124-acre) national park is one of the least visited in Costa Rica. Its peak sits at 3328m (10,919ft) above sea level and shares its foundation with Volcán Irazú, so that they are often described as 'twin volcanoes'. It gets its name from *torre alba* or 'white smoke' – a term coined by the early Spanish settlers. There are three recognizable craters. The central crater is the deepest, dropping 50m (164ft). There are also two old cones on its slopes. The last major eruptions occurred in 1866 and current activity consists of steam and gas eruptions leaving sulphur deposits. There are a number of hiking trails in the park and once on the crater rim there are superb 360° views. The upper slopes are clothed with premontane forest, with rainforest lower down full of ferns, bamboos and bromeliads. There is a wide variety of birds and other wildlife. There is no ranger station, but the Volcán Turrialba Lodge, just outside the park, offers organized tours.

Volcán Tenorio National Park

Located in the Guanacaste Cordillera, Tenorio is one of the newest of Costa Rica's national parks, and its trails have already become popular with hikers. The park protects the watershed of Tenorio Volcano, which rises to 1916m (6286ft). The volcano is extinct, but there is a stunning crater lake to admire. It is surrounded by 12,871ha (31,800 acres) of mixed forest, some of which is primary, drained by the dazzling Río Celeste, its blue waters formed by mineral deposits within the park. There are

Volcán Turrialba National Park

Location: 44 miles (71 km) east of San José, in Cartago province.

Size: 1257ha (4124 acres).

Altitude: Up to 3328m (10,919ft).

Climate: Average temperature is 15.5°C (60°F); rainfall 3500mm (138in) annually.

Of Interest: Volcanic features; premontane and rainforest.

Accommodation: None in the park, but it is well within reach of the hotels in San José.

Volcán Tenorio National Park

Location: Close to the town of Bijagua, Guanacaste province.

Size: 12,872ha (31,800 acres).

Altitude: Up to 1916m (6286ft).

Climate: Forms a barrier to the trade winds, with clouds on the Atlantic slope and clearer skies on the Pacific slope. Average rainfall 4000mm (158in) a year; average temperature 24°C (75°F).

Of Interest: Volcanic features; various forms of forest, with a good range of wildlife.

Central Volcanic Conservation Area

Braulio Carrillo

The national park was named after Costa Rica's third president, who at one stage declared himself to be 'President for Life' – although he didn't last for long. Braulio Carrillo was one of the earliest promoters of the coffee industry and he proposed that a road should be built from the Central Valley to the Caribbean coast so that coffee beans could be taken to the markets in Europe much more quickly than on the existing route via Puntarenas on the Pacific coast and the treacherous Cape Horn. In the event, only a cobblestone path was built to take the ox carts loaded with coffee beans and even this was superceded in 1885 when the railroad from San José to Puerto Limón was constructed. It was not until 1985 that the Guápiles Highway was finally built.

wide-ranging views from the summit taking in Lake Nicaragua, Arenal Volcano and the northern lowlands. The forest areas are rich in plants such as palms, ferns, bromeliads, orchids and heliconias, while its wildlife includes three types of monkey, Baird's Tapir and birds such as trogons and hawks.

Accommodation

None within the park boundaries, but nearby are:
Heliconias Lodge, tel: 2286 4203. Simple lodgings in cabins on the lower slopes of the volcano.
La Carolina, 6km (3.7 miles) north of Bijagua, tel: 2380 1656, www.lacarolinalodge.com Set on a working ranch, the price includes three meals. Guided treks and horse riding on offer.

Iguanas

Costa Rica provides a home for 68 lizard species, of which 38 are classed as iguanas. The species that will be most familiar to ecotourists are the Green Iguana (*Iguana iguana*) and the Black Iguana (*Ctenosaura similis*). The Green Iguana is the larger and more widespread of the two and can grow up to 2m (6.5ft) in length. Looking dragon-like, they are often found in trees along river banks throughout much of Costa Rica at low to middle altitudes. Iguanas are sluggish creatures and rarely make any agitated movements. The adults are largely herbivores, feeding on leaves and small twigs, but immature iguanas take a variety of insects. Although predominantly green, they have the ability to change colour according to their background. The males, in particular, are adorned with spines, crests and throat fans. They will defend a territory in which there may be as many as four females.

The Green Iguana breeds in the early part of the dry season, laying up to 40 eggs in a burrow. The hatchlings are vulnerable to predators and may be taken by a variety of birds and animals. The Black Iguana or Ctenosaur is only found on the drier Pacific slope and rarely by rivers. Another variety is the Green Marine Iguana, which grazes on algae in rock pools on the south Pacific coast.

Iguanas can become very tame and in some hotel grounds they will take food from the hand. They have always been hunted for their meat, which although an acquired taste, is said to resemble chicken. Iguana Park, near Orotina in Puntarenas province, is a non-profit making organization, which raises Green Iguanas in captivity, selling some for their meat, but releasing the majority to the wild.

Braulio Carrillo National Park

When it was decided to construct a new highway from San José to Puerto Limón on the Caribbean coast via Guápiles, environmentalists were concerned that the virgin rain- and cloud forest on the eastern watershed of the Central Valley would be under threat. It would be easy to imagine ribbon development of motels, sodas (similar to American diners), filling stations and settlement lining the road and ruining the environment. In 1978 it was therefore decided to set up the Braulio Carrillo National Park, named after one of the country's 19th-century presidents (see panel, page 124).

Covering some 46,000ha (113,666 acres), the park includes a range of five altitudinal life zones and holds a tremendous variety of fauna and flora. The new highway effectively cuts the park in two, but gives an excellent opportunity to get a flavour of the area, with luxuriant vegetation draped with epiphytes and lianas visible through the mist, along with foaming waterfalls and vast tracts of Gunnera, which, with its massive leaves, is known as 'the poor man's umbrella'. As the road nears the Caribbean coastal plain, look out for the Río Sucio Bridge. The view upstream shows the confluence of the Río Sucio (the name means 'dirty river') and the Río Hondura, which is a crystal clear mountain stream. The Sucio, on the other hand, has its headwaters on the ash-covered slopes of Volcán Irazú, turning the water a reddish brown.

Braulio Carrillo National Park contains 84% of primary forest and altitude-wise it ranges from 36m (118ft) at La Selva to 2906m (9535ft) at the summit of Volcán Barva, the greatest altitudinal range of any Costa Rican national park. Rainfall and temperature correspondingly vary greatly. The range of wildlife is staggering. It is estimated that the forest contains around 6000 species of plants, with 600 trees, providing a habitat for more than 500 species of birds, including rarities such as the Resplendent Quetzal, King Vulture, most of the toucan family, the Bare-necked Umbrellabird,

Braulio Carrillo National Park

Location: 20km (12 miles) northeast of San José.
Size: 46,000ha (113,666 acres).
Altitude: 36m (118ft) to 2906m (9535ft) at the summit of Volcán Barva.
Climate: Hot and humid on the lower levels of the Caribbean slope. Cold on the higher levels with frost not unknown. Average annual rainfall is 457cm (180in).
Of Interest: Volcanic features, rainforest, cloud forest, wide range of birds, mammals and butterflies.
Accommodation: There are no lodgings or camp sites within the park boundaries, but plenty of choice in nearby San José.

Central Volcanic Conservation Area

Flame-throated Warbler, Black-crowned Antpitta and a vast range of hummingbirds, trogons and parrots. Amongst the mammals, there are three types of monkey, numerous felines such as Jaguar, Ocelot and Puma, Baird's Tapir, Pacas, Raccoons and Peccaries. Butterflies abound and you would be unlucky not to see Blue Morphos, Magnificent Owls, Zebra Longwings and Swallowtails. Hikers should beware of snakes – the park contains two of the most venomous: the Bushmaster and the Fer-de-lance.

For administrative purposes, Braulio Carrillo National Park is divided into two sections – the Quebrada González sector and the Barva Volcano sector.

The Quebrada González Sector

This part of the park is bisected by the Guápiles Highway. There are two ranger stations. The Zurquí station is just past the road tunnel of the same name. There is an information centre and three short trails, varying from 1–3km (0.6–1.9 miles) in length. The Carillo ranger station is a further 22km (14 miles) along the road, close to the toll booth in the centre of the road. Here there are two further trails. One, named La Botella, leads to waterfalls and a view down the Patria Canyon.

Right: The Aerial Tram at Braulio Carrillo gives fine views of the wildlife of the rainforest canopy.

Braulio Carrillo National Park

The Rainforest Aerial Tram

Located just outside the Braulio Carrillo National Park, the Aerial Tram is the brainchild of the American naturalist Dr Donald Perry, who developed the idea after extensive research at Rara Avis (see panel, page 54). Basically, the Aerial Tram consists of 20 open-air cable cars, each carrying four passengers and a naturalist guide, travelling at various levels though the forest, starting in the understorey and lower canopy and returning at the upper canopy level – a 2.6km (1.6-mile) tour. The guides are equipped with walkie-talkies and if one spots something interesting, it is passed on to the others, so that all the passengers benefit. This is a wonderful way of seeing the vegetation and wildlife of the forest canopy and good views are guaranteed of epiphytes, butterflies and birds, but don't go there with preconceived ideas of what you will see – anything (or nothing) might turn up. The best chance of seeing wildlife is early in the morning before tour groups arrive.

The building of the aerial tram was in itself an ecological achievement and the construction firm were obliged to bring in material on foot or by helicopter to avoid damaging the habitats. The tram is not cheap, but for many visitors this will be the highlight of their time in Costa Rica. There is a private reserve of 400ha (988 acres) surrounding the aerial tram, with a few short trails, plus an information centre, which shows a video detailing the history of the development. There is a secure car park, from where a shuttle takes visitors to the centre; tel: 2257 5961, www.rainforesttram.com

The Barva Volcano Sector

This part of the Braulio Carrillo National Park has to be approached from a different direction. The road from San José winds through coffee plantations and dairy farms to the village of Sacramento, where the paved road ends. From here there is a rough track to the Barva Ranger Station. A 3km (1.9-mile) trail leads up through deciduous forest and cloud forest to the summit of Volcán Barva. The volcano is extinct, but there is an impressive crater filled with a blue-green lake. Unlike the Poás and Irazú volcanoes, the crater rim has epiphyte-laden cloud forest trees, with a range of highland forest birds, including the Resplendent Quetzal, Long-tailed Silky Flycatcher, Flame-throated Warbler and Golden-browed Chlorophonia. For the really intrepid hiker there is a 30km

Safety

Braulio Carrillo is probably the only national park in Costa Rica where crime is a problem. You are advised to leave your vehicle in the protected car parks at the ranger stations. Any car left at the roadside is likely to be broken into and any valuables stolen. There have also been examples of hikers being subjected to armed robberies. It must be stressed, however, that these have been isolated instances. On the more remote trails it is advisable to be accompanied by a ranger.

Central Volcanic Conservation Area

Lankester Botanical Gardens

Location: 5km (3.7 miles) east of Cartago, on the road to Paraíso.
Size: 10.7ha (26 acres).
Climate: Warm and mild throughout the year, with rainy season from May to November.
Of Interest: Trees and gardens with special collections of orchids and epiphytes.

(19-mile) trail from the top of Volcán Barva to La Selva Biological Station, involving a descent of some 3000m (9843ft). This could take about four days and hiring a guide is strongly recommended.

Getting There

Take the Guápiles Highway from San José to the Quesada González sector. There is a service bus from San José. You will have to flag the bus down on the return journey and it may not stop if it is full. For the Barva Volcano sector, drive through Heredia, turning off to Barva, San José de la Montaña and Sacramento. Thence take a rough track to the ranger station. All three ranger stations are open from 08:00 to 16:00.

The Bare-necked Umbrellabird

A bird that many bird-watchers would wish to see in Costa Rica is the Bare-necked Umbrellabird, if only because of its rarity – it is only seen in Costa Rica and the western side of neighbouring Panama. The Braulio Carrillo National Park is as good a spot as any to see this remarkable bird, which spends much of the year in the foothills of the Caribbean slope before migrating upslope to breed locally in the forests between 800m (2600ft) and 2000m (6500ft). It is a large bird, basically black, with a heavy, broad bill and huge head made to appear larger in the male by an umbrella-shaped crest. The throat has a skin of bright scarlet that the male is able to inflate in courtship display and there are small orange bare patches on each side of the foreneck. The display also includes a

Right: Lankester Botanical Gardens are famed for their outstanding orchid collection.

Lankester Botanical Gardens

far-sounding booming noise that has been likened to a mallet striking an oildrum. The umbrellabird inhabits the mid canopy of primary forests, where it feeds on fruits and insects. It will also catch frogs and small lizards, which it kills by beating them on branches.

Lankester Botanical Gardens

The area to the southeast of Cartago is one of the most attractive parts of the Central Valley, and it is here, just past the village of Paraíso, that we find the world-renowned Lankester Gardens, where orchids are the main attraction. They were originally the private collection of Charles Lankester, an English biologist who arrived in Costa Rica to work in coffee production. He established the gardens in 1917, with the aim of preserving a collection of Central American native species. When he died the gardens were acquired by the North American Orchid Society and the English Stanley Smith Foundation, who, in 1971, passed it on to the University of Costa Rica, which administers it today. The 10.7ha (26 acres) of gardens and forest are famed for their orchids (there are over 8000 on show), but there are also collections of bromeliads, bamboos, cacti and a vast number of epiphytes, with around 3000 species of plants, mostly from Costa Rica and other Central American countries. Particularly attractive are the heliconias, with their brightly coloured flowers pollinated by hummingbirds, and similar species such as birds of paradise, Marantaceae, Musaceae, gingers and *Costus*. Bromeliads are one of the plant groups that are best adapted to the Gardens' climatic conditions. Most of the members of this family are easily recognized by the arrangement of their leaves into a rosette and their colourful blossoms. There are around 200 native bromeliad species in Costa Rica and many of the trees in the Gardens are frequently covered with *Tillandsia* genus bromeliads.

With such a wealth of plants and blossoms, Lankester Gardens are highly attractive to birds and butterflies – over 100 species of birds have been recorded and the Gardens have been declared a refuge for migratory birds. The orchid blossoms are at their peak from February to April, but there is plenty to see throughout the year. There is an admission charge. The Gardens are open daily 08:30–15:30, except bank holidays; tel: 2552 3247, www.jardinbotanicolankester.com

Orchids

It is surprisingly difficult to spot Costa Rican orchids in the wild as they are epiphytic and often grow high up in the canopy, and may only actually flower for a few days at a time. Fortunately, Lankester Gardens have a wonderful collection of orchids that are frequently displayed at eye level. Costa Rica is home to around 1400 orchid species of which 20% are endemic. Orchids get their name from the Greek *orchis*, meaning testicles – which may have something to do with the fact that terrestrial orchids have two bulbs or corms. Orchids are, in fact, quite cosmopolitan, growing in almost every habitat except glaciers and deserts. In temperate countries, most orchids are terrestrial, but in tropical and subtropical areas they are epiphytic, living on trees. Orchids as a group are identified by the fact that they are bilaterally symmetrical, resupinate (appearing to be upside down), have a petal that is always highly modified, have stamens and carpels that are fused, and have seeds that are minute.

Central Volcanic Conservation Area

Getting There
Buses leave Cartago for Paraíso every 30 minutes. Disembark at the electricity station. From there it is a walk of 600m (656yd).

Accommodation
The gardens do not provide accommodation, nor is there much to choose from in Cartago. Try:

Sanchiri Mirador and Lodge, south of Paraíso, tel: 2574 5454, www.sanchiri.com This delightful restaurant perched on a ridge overlooking the Orosí Valley serves good local food. It also has a number of rustic cabins with private facilities and stunning views.

Common Birds of the Central Valley
There is plenty of interest for the bird-watcher in the Central Valley of Costa Rica, even within the boundaries of Greater San José. This is particularly true in winter, when there are many migrants from North America. The skies are full of Black and Turkey Vultures swirling around in the thermals, while the telephone wires make a good perch for birds of the flycatcher family, such as the Great Kiskadee, Western and Gray Kingbirds, and Social Flycatcher. Red-tailed and Roadside Hawks also use the wires for lookout points.

In the fields, farm animals are invariably followed by Cattle Egrets, while suburban parks usually have groups of noisy Grackles. Garden birds include the national bird, the Clay-coloured Robin, and the rather attractive Rufous-collared Sparrow.

Guayabo National Monument
Some 19km (12 miles) east of the town of Turrialba is Costa Rica's premier archaeological site. Although Guayabo cannot be compared with some of the Aztec and Maya sites further north in Central America, it is nevertheless of great importance as it gives a fascinating insight into the way of life of the people who lived here in pre-Columbian times as long as 2500 years ago. The site was discovered in the late 1880s, probably by colonists clearing the land for coffee plantations. The first excavations were done by Anastasio Alfaro, who was director of the National Museum at that time. After these initial digs there was no further work here

CATIE

Keen gardeners and environmentalists will certainly want to visit the **Centro Agrónomico Tropical de Investigación y Enseñanza** (CATIE). Located 5km (3 miles) southeast of Turrialba on the road to Siquirres, it is one of the world's most important centres for research into the development of tropical agriculture. Research on coffee dominates. The centre covers 880ha (2174 acres) of beautifully landscaped grounds including an ornamental lake, with trails providing rewarding birding. The best way to visit CATIE is to join a group tour from San José.

Guayabo National Monument

until 1968, when Carlos Aguilar, working through the University of Costa Rica, reopened the site. Realizing its importance, the government made Guayabo a protected site in 1973. The main problem is shortage of funds and as the initial US grant has dwindled away, the future looks bleak. The site covers some 20ha (50 acres), of which only about one tenth has been excavated. What has emerged is a township that may have supported as many as 10,000 people up to around AD1400, after which the site was abandoned. The reason why is not clear. It could have been an epidemic or perhaps a war with a neighbouring tribe. The excavations have revealed paved roads, houses, temple foundations, burial sites and bridges. It is clear that the inhabitants were skilful in water management, having built aqueducts (some still functioning) and water storage tanks. They were also able to bring large stones from some distance, some of which bear petroglyphs showing an Alligator and a Jaguar, suggesting a primitive form of written language. The more valuable gold and ceramic artefacts found on the site are now in the Museo Nacional in San José.

The fact that the surrounding land is protected has fortunately meant that a sizeable chunk of pre-montane forest has survived on the site, supporting a rich and varied bird life. The colonial nests of Montezuma Oropendola are common, and hummingbirds such as the Crowned Woodnymph and Rufous-crested Coquette have been noted, along with the Green Honeycreeper and the Collared Aricari of the toucan family. Other wildlife includes the Nine-banded Armadillo and Blue Morpho butterfly, and there is a good variety of orchids.

There is a ranger station, an exhibition area full of pre-Columbian artefacts found on the site, plus camping and picnic areas. Guayabo is open daily 08:00–16:00 and a national park entrance fee is payable.

Accommodation

Camping is permitted at the site. The nearest hotels are in Turrialba. A lodge close to the site is:
La Calzada Lodge, Apdo. 260, Turrialba, tel: 2253 0465. Small wooden hotel with seven rooms and a thatched restaurant. Local tours arranged.

Guayabo National Monument

Location: 19km (12 miles) east of the town of Turrialba.
Size: 20ha (50 acres), plus a further protected area of forest.
Altitude: 850–1000m (2789–3281ft).
Climate: Generally mild with abundant rainfall giving pre-montane rainforest.
Of Interest: Pre-Columbian remains. Rainforest wildlife.

Getting There

Head for the town of Turrialba 65km (40 miles) east of San José. From here it is 19km (12 miles) to Guayabo.

HIGHLAND CONSERVATION AREA

This conservation area covers the southern spine of the country marked by the Cordillera de Talamanca, which has no recent record of volcanic activity. The Tapantí National Park lies on the northern slope of the mountain chain, marking the watershed of the Orosí Valley complex with its hydroelectric schemes. Just to the south is the infamous Cerro de la Muerte where the Pan-American Highway is at its highest point, crossing a dangerous, cloudy mountain pass. This leads to the Chirripó National Park, named after Costa Rica's highest mountain, Mount Chirripó, which rises to 3820m (12,533ft). This national park joins on to La Amistad International Park, which continues over the Panamanian border.

Highland Conservation Area Top Ten

Puma
Jaguar
Brocket Deer
Anteaters
Glacial features on Mount Chirripó
Baird's Tapir
Resplendent Quetzal
Three-wattled Bellbird
Possible home of the Harpy Eagle
Heliconias at Wilson Gardens

Opposite, top to bottom: A Puma and her kitten (Pumas are also known as Mountain Lions, Cougars and Panthers); River Otters are common in the lowland waterways of Costa Rica; Water Lily growing in the one of the ponds at the Wilson Botanical Gardens, developed on the site of an abandoned coffee plantation.

Highland Conservation Area

Tapantí National Park

Tapantí National Park

Location: 27km (16 miles) southeast of Cartago.

Size: 6080ha (15,023 acres).

Altitude: 1220m (4000ft) to 2560m (8400ft).

Climate: Probably the wettest national park in the country, with 8375mm (330in) of rainfall. Average temperature is 20°C (68°F).

Of Interest: Upland rainforest, with luxuriant vegetation and rich wildlife.

Getting There: From San José, take the Pan-American Highway to Cartago and then Highway 10 to Paraíso. Follow the Orosí signs and then those for Tapantí. The last stretch of road is in bad condition. The public bus only goes as far as the village of Río Macho, which is 9km (5.6 miles) away from the park entrance. Park staff can radio for a taxi for the return journey.

Accommodation: La Esperanza de El Guarco Biological Station is in the Tapantí National Park and has simple lodging for up to 15 people.

Tapantí lies along the northern slopes of the Cordillera de Talamanca and claims to have the highest rainfall in the country – 8375mm (330in). Not surprisingly, the park is bisected by nearly 150 rivers and fast-flowing streams that have attracted hydroelectric schemes at lower levels, which involved constructing roads through this previously inaccessible area. To protect the watershed and to prevent ribbon development along the road, the area was created a national wildlife refuge in 1982 and updated to national park status in 1994. Tapantí rises from1220m (4000ft) to 2560m (8400ft) above sea level and contains two life zones – lower montane rainforest and premontane rainforest. The forest areas are noted for their profusion of epiphytes, with orchids particularly abundant and in flower at all times of the year. Tree ferns, bromeliads, mosses, lichens, Gunnera and lianas complete the biomass. Many mammals inhabit the park although, as usual, they are difficult to spot. Amongst the 45 species are Baird's Tapir, River Otters, Brocket Deer, Jaguar, Ocelot, Jaguarundi, Howler Monkeys and Silky Anteaters. Birds are more obvious and over 260 species have been recorded, including the Resplendent Quetzal, which is frequently seen near the ranger station. Others include both types of oropendula, various woodpeckers and rarities such as Spotted Woodcreeper, the gaudy Redheaded Barbet, Spangled-cheeked Tanager and Spotted Barbtail. Numerous varieties of hummingbird can be seen feeding on the flowering epiphytes.

When visiting Tapantí, remember that mornings can be quite pleasant and sunny, but it soon clouds over and by midday the rain arrives, so wet-weather gear is advisable. The ranger station at Tapantí is open from 07:00 until 17:00 and has a small nature display and gift shop. A number of well-marked trails start at the ranger station. The Oropendula and Pantanoso trails lead to a swimming area with picnic tables, while La Pava trail takes you to a couple of waterfalls.

Anteaters

Surprisingly, the anteaters are related to both the sloths and armadillos, belonging to the order *Edentata* (meaning 'without teeth'). There are four species of anteater, three of which occur

Tapantí National Park

in Costa Rica. The Giant Anteater is extremely rare and may even be extinct in the country. Smaller is the Northern Tamandua, while the Silky Anteater is tinier still. As the silky anteater is nocturnal, visitors are more likely to see the Northern Tamandua. Anteaters are highly specialized to feed on termites and ants. They have strong front claws to break up ant and termite colonies and long thin snouts to get into the nests. They have long tongues coated with a sticky saliva to catch the insects. Anteaters nest in hollows in trees producing one baby at a time, which will often ride on the mother's back. Breeding takes place at any time during the year. It seems strange that all three varieties of anteater can coexist in the same stretch of forest, particularly as they all eat the same type of food. It is suggested that their activity pattern may reduce competition. Silky Anteaters, for example, are strictly nocturnal, while the other two species are also active during the day. In addition, the Giant Anteater is ground dwelling, while the Silky Anteater is arboreal and the Tamandua is happy in both environments.

Chirripó National Park

The centrepiece of this high-elevation national park is Mount Chirripó, Costa Rica's highest mountain, which reaches 3820m (12,533ft). The park covers 50,150ha (123,918 acres) and a great deal of this area rarely sees a human being, much to the benefit of the wildlife. One extremely remote part of the park is known as the 'Savannah of the Lions' – a reference to the large number of Pumas known to exist here. A number of life zones can be identified, differentiated largely by altitude. Some 25,000 years ago

Tapantí and Chirripó National Parks

Chirripó National Park

Location: 20km (12 miles) northeast of San Isidro. Covers parts of San José, Limón and Cartago provinces.
Size: 50,150ha (123,918 acres).
Altitude: From 900m (3000ft) to 3820m (12,533ft).
Climate: Ranges widely with elevation. Cold and windy on the summit. Warm and humid at lower levels, up to 3800mm (150in) precipitation, with driest months March and April.
Of Interest: Costa Rica's highest mountain, cloud and mixed rainforest and páramo, with abundant wildlife.

Highland Conservation Area

Getting There

Take the Pan-American Highway from San José to Cartago, then continue to San Isidro de El General. From there take the road that leads to the small town of San Gerardo de Rivas. Service buses go to this town. The ranger station is just south of San Gerardo.

the summit was covered with glacial ice and the highest levels today are marked by bare rock with glacial features such as U-shaped valleys, ribbon lakes and moraine deposits, with biting winds and temperatures that frequently drop to minus 10°C, belying the fact that this is a mere 9° north of the Equator. Below this is a type of tundra, the alpine páramo – a strange area of high moorland with clumpy grassland and stunted dwarf trees, a habitat that is vulnerable to fire caused by the drying winds. At lower levels, there are oak, mixed and cloud forest sections, with an understorey of ferns and bamboo, which are rich in flora and fauna. Some of the oak trees are magnificent specimens reaching 30m (100ft). There are thought to be healthy numbers of Baird's Tapirs and Jaguars in the forests, although they are rarely seen. Spider Monkeys are more obvious. Over 400 species of bird have been recorded and there are good numbers of trogons, woodpeckers and woodcreepers. Chirripó was considered a sacred mountain by the pre-Columbian Indians, although it is believed that only the tribal leaders and shamans were allowed to the summit. Some curious rock formations known as Los Crestones were treated as a shrine.

Pumas

The Puma (*Puma concolor*) is also known as the Cougar, Mountain Lion and Panther. It is confined to the Americas, where it is the most widely distributed of the cat family, extending from Alaska in the north to the southern Andes. It is also seen in a wide variety of habitats, though in Costa Rica it is generally found in remote forested areas with dense undergrowth, such as in the Chirripó National Park, where one area is known as the Sabana de los Leones (the Savannah of the Lions) after the large population of Pumas. It is the second largest of the cat family in the New World after the Jaguar. The Puma stalks and ambushes its prey, which, in Costa Rica, is often the White-tailed or Brocket Deer, although it has been known to take domestic animals and will take smaller prey if necessary. Adults stand at about 60cm (2ft) to 80cm (2.7ft) at the shoulders, while from nose to tail they can measure 2.4m (8ft), with females generally smaller than the males. Unlike lions, they do not roar, but have a variety of grunts, hisses and purrs. The Puma's coat is typically tawny grey, without spots or stripes. It has, proportionately, the longest legs in the cat family, giving it great leaping and short sprint capability. Pumas are solitary animals, but the female will stay with her kittens for up to six months. As many as six kittens may be born although the norm is two or three, with the survival rate estimated to be one per litter. Owing to their secretive nature, the number of Pumas in Costa Rica is unknown, but it is generally considered to be 'near threatened' or 'vulnerable'. Although there have been reports of Pumas attacking humans in the United States, there have been no instances in Costa Rica. Because they are timid, it is unlikely that you would encounter a Puma on a forest trail, but if you do meet one, wave your arms and shout. Do not run away, as this may provoke the Puma to chase.

Accommodation

Camping is not allowed within the park. Lodge accommodation is available in the *refugios* for hikers. The following is recommended for hikers in San Gerardo:

Posada del Descanso (no phone). Lodgings in a private house, owned by a local family whose members regularly take part in the Chirripó marathon and are a fund of information on local activities.

Hotel Los Crestones,
south of the plaza,
San Gerardo de Rivas,
tel: 2770 1200
www.hotelloscrestones.com
Small, comfortable hotel,
convenient for birders and hikers.

Climbing Mount Chirripó

If you wish to climb Mount Chirripó, you will have to do some advance planning. You need to contact the National Parks Service to book a place, as only a certain number of people are allowed on the trail each day and the climb is very popular in the dry season. You should register with the ranger station on arrival. Camping is not allowed in the park and fires are banned, so sufficient food and water must be taken. Although the climb is straightforward and does not require any rock-climbing skills, it is a long uphill drag and the complete hike there and back normally takes two or three days. Accommodation needs to be booked at the simple refuge huts, so a good sleeping bag is needed. Bear in mind the climate and adopt a layered approach to clothing. It can

Opposite: Baird's Trogon. There are 10 varieties of trogon to be found in Costa Rica – all are colourful and exotic.

Highland Conservation Area

La Amistad International Park

Location: Talamanca Cordillera, extending over the border into Panama.
Size: 194,000ha (479,000 acres).
Altitude: 150m (490ft) rising to 3554m (11,660ft).
Climate: Varies with altitude. Hot and humid at lower levels with average temperatures around 26°C (79°F). February and March are the driest months. It is cold on the summits, with snow and frost not unknown.
Of Interest: Wide range of life zones varying from tropical rainforest to alpine páramo, supporting an incredible selection of wildlife, much of it rare and endangered.
Getting There: Pan-American Highway from San José to San Isidro el General (152km/92 miles). Continue to the Panamanian border. Access points on the left-hand side of the road with three ranger stations.
Accommodation: Camping allowed at two of the ranger stations, but there are few facilities and no other accommodation within the park. La Amistad Lodge, tel: 2221 8634, adjoins the park near the Panama border. It is a working farm with a private wildlife reserve, 10 rooms and a cosy restaurant. Guided hiking and horse-riding tours offered.

be quite hot at lower levels and rain can be expected anywhere, even in the dry season. The summit can be extremely cold, but with the clear air, a sun block is advisable. Also take sunglasses, first-aid kit, insect repellent and a torch – the refuges have no lights. The hike begins at around 1219m (4000ft), passing through pastureland and then thick cloud forest. About halfway to the huts is an open-sided rest station, which should only be used for accommodation in an emergency. After 14km (8.7 miles) the accommodation huts are reached, surrounded by a swampy, treeless grassland. The following morning, it is a 90-minute walk to the summit of Mount Chirripó. There is a choice of spending the day around the summit area and returning to the huts for the night or making the descent on the same day. With luck there will be clear visibility and views of both the Pacific and the Caribbean.

La Amistad International Park

This 194,000ha (479,000-acre) friendship park extends into neighbouring Panama. Together with a number of other parks, reserves and Indian reservations, it forms the 600,000ha (1,482,000-acre) La Amistad Biosphere Reserve, a UNESCO World Heritage Site. The park covers much of the non-volcanic Talamanca Cordillera, rising from 150m (490ft) on the Caribbean side to 3554m (11,660ft) at the highest point. La Amistad covers eight life zones from tropical lowland rainforest to cloud forest and the alpine páramo. Much of the park is unexplored and although there are three ranger stations on the Pacific side, they are frequently unmanned. There are a few trails, but they are often overgrown and badly marked. It would be foolhardy to venture far into the park without a guide. Because of the remote and virgin landscape, the wildlife statistics (mostly 'guesstimates') are mind-blowing. It is thought that up to two-thirds of all of Costa Rica's species are found at La Amistad, including a large number of its endangered species and many endemics. All six neotropical cats (Jaguar, Puma, Ocelot, Margay, Jaguarundi and Oncilla) live here, along with the rare Baird's Tapir, Coatis, Giant Anteaters and monkeys.

A staggering 600 species of birds have been identified, including the country's largest number of Resplendent Quetzals, the Three-wattled Bellbird, and the Umbrellabird. This may also be the last stronghold of the Harpy Eagle, although many ornithologists consider that it

La Amistad International Park

may be extinct in Costa Rica. There are also 115 species of fish, 300 reptiles and amphibians and over 9000 flowering plant species – and more are being discovered all the time!

In January 2008, scientists from London's Natural History Museum, working with colleagues from Costa Rica and Panama, announced that they had discovered eleven previously unknown plant and animal species in La Amistad park. Amongst the six plants was a

Highland Conservation Area

Location: Southern Puntarenas province, 300km (186 miles) southeast of San José.

Size: 266ha (657 acres).

Altitude: 1120m (3674ft) to 1385m (4543ft).

Climate: Cool, with temperatures averaging 21°C (70°F) during the day and 15°C (60°F) at night. Rain, generally in intermittent showers, is likely in the afternoons or evenings from April to December, with 4000mm (158in) of rain annually.

Of Interest: Subtropical gardens and rainforest, with rare and endangered plants.

mistletoe with what they described as a 'spectacular yellow and red flower'. Also discovered were three salamanders and two frogs. The salamanders, one of which was a dwarf species under an inch long, were of particular interest, as they had 'ballistic' tongues, which could shoot out, catch an insect and withdraw back into the mouth in seven milliseconds. The expeditions are part of the Darwin Initiative, funded by the British Government.

Wilson Botanical Gardens (Las Cruces Biological Station)

Robert and Catherine Wilson, former owners of Fantastic Gardens in Miami, decided in 1958 to relocate to Costa Rica. They bought an abandoned coffee plantation at San Vito de Coto Brus with the idea of growing tea plants. They soon decided, however, to devote themselves to the cultivation of ornamental and tropical plants. With the help of the Brazilian landscape architect Roberto Burle Marx, these magnificent botanical gardens gradually evolved, with more than 1000 genera in 212 plant families. Paths and trails imaginatively wind around hillsides through wild and apparently cultivated areas, with ferns, aroids, bromeliads, gingers, heliconias, marantas and palms. Visitors particularly enjoy the Orchid Trail, Tree Fern Hill, and the Hummingbird Garden. The gardens are rich in native plants and animals, with 320 species of birds recorded. Bird-watchers are delighted to see, for example, Scarlet-thighed Dacnis, Silver-throated Tanagers, Violaceous Trogons, Blue-headed Parrots, Sabre-winged Hummingbirds, Turquiose Cotingas and many more. There are also over 800 species of butterflies and moths and numerous amphibians and reptiles. Over 100 species of mammals have been seen, 43 of which are bats.

In 1973, the gardens and the adjacent 145ha (360-acre) forest reserve were taken over by the Organization for Tropical Studies (the OTS also runs La Selva and Palo Verde biological stations). The organization dedicates itself to teaching, research and on-site scientific training. Plants are propagated for horticulture, and species threatened with habitat loss are maintained and kept for reforestation projects. There is plenty of accommodation available, both for resident scientists and for visiting birding and natural history groups, while day visitors are welcome. They can follow self-guided trails or hire a resident naturalist guide. There is a restaurant serving locally grown food, a gift shop and a library. The gardens are open 08:00–16:00, closed Monday; tel: 2773 3278, www.esintro.co.cr

Getting There

Take the Pan-American Highway south from San José. The nearest settlement is San Vito, from where local buses stop outside Wilson Botanical Gardens.

Accommodation

Las Cruces Biological Station (www.ots.duke.edu/en/lascruces) has accommodation in the form of 12 attractive cabins with private facilities and balcony. The price includes three meals per day at the reserve restaurant and one daily guided walk.

Rainforests and the Logging Industry

Costa Rica's rainforests, like those of many other countries, face a serious threat from the logging industry. Despite the fact that so much of the country is protected, illegal logging still takes place in the more remote national parks, due to the fact that the NPS does not have the manpower resources to police such wide areas. The loggers target the mature hardwood trees of the forest, such as Cristobal, Mahogany and Nazareno. As well as depriving the forests of their mature trees, the removal of timber can destroy vast swathes of valuable habitat. The government has often claimed that there is a balance between deforestation and reforestation, but recent figures dispute this. In addition, some recent research claims that primary rainforest is irreplaceable and even if felled forest areas are replaced with faster growing plants they will not be as efficient at soaking up carbon dioxide or providing homes for the creatures that live there. The loss of habitat means that up to a quarter of the species found in the rainforest could be lost.

There are no laws in Costa Rica to prevent small landowners from selling timber on their land and, particularly where unemployment is a problem, the inducements of the woodcutters has been hard to resist. A further problem when rainforest areas are stripped is that the lack of trees speeds up run-off from rainfall causing erosion of hill slopes and the pollution of rivers.

NATIONAL PARKS GUIDE

List of National Parks and Other Reserves

The North Caribbean Conservation Area
Tortuguero National Park – Tropical lowland rainforest; waterways and creeks; turtle-nesting beaches.
Barra del Colorado National Wildlife Refuge – Tropical lowland rainforest; delta and creeks; sport fishing.
Other protected areas:
Matina Forest Reserve
Pacuare Protected Area

The South Caribbean Conservation Area
Cahuita National Park – Coral reef; coastal mangroves and forest.
Gandoca-Manzanillo National Wildlife Refuge – Coral reef; turtle-nesting beach; lowland rainforest.
Hitoy-Cerere Biological Reserve – Tropical rainforest.
Other protected areas:
Aviarios del Caribe
Río Banana Protected Area

The Northern Conservation Zone
Arenal Volcano National Park – Volcanic features.
La Selva Biological Research Station – Rainforest research station with trails.
Rara Avis – Private rainforest reserve.
Caño Negro National Wildlife Refuge – Lagoons, pools and river channel.
Monteverde Cloud Forest Reserve – Private cloud forest reserve.
Santa Elena Cloud Forest Reserve – Largely primary forest in private cloud forest reserve.
Children's Eternal Rain Forest – Private cloud forest reserve.
Other protected area:
San Ramón Protected Area

The Guanacaste Conservation Zone
Santa Rosa National Park – Tropical dry forest; turtle-nesting

Public Holidays and Festivals (Jan–May)

1 January – *Año Nuevo* (New Year's Day).
Mid-January – *Fiesta de Santa Cruz* in the Nicoya Peninsula. Rodeos, music and dancing.
March/April – *Semana Santa* (Easter Week).
11 April – *Día de Juan Santamaría* (Juan Santamaría Day). Anniversary of the Battle of Rivas and the day of the National Hero.
1 May – *Día del Trabajo* (Labour Day).

Opposite, top to bottom:
Rainforest scene in the Braulio Carrillo National Park; Ringed Kingfisher, the most common and widespread of the six kingfisher species found in Costa Rica; typical Pacific coast beach at the Tango Mar resort.

National Parks Guide

Pamphlets

Some glossy pamphlets available: *Costa Rica Wildlife – An Introduction to Familiar Species*. A Pocket Naturalist's guide. Waterford Press. **Rainforest Publications** produce a number of handy, pocket-sized identification charts, covering general wildlife, cloud forest and highland birds, birds of the Atlantic lowlands and the Caribbean coast, and Pacific coast reef fish.

beach; historical interest.
Guanacaste National Park – Dry forest, cloud forest and rainforest; dry plains.
Rincón de la Vieja National Park – Volcanic features; dry forest; rainforest; waterfalls.
Other protected area:
Miravalles Protected Area

The North Pacific Coastal Conservation Area
Isla Bolaños Biological Reserve – Sea-bird nesting sites.
Las Baulas National Marine Park – Turtle-nesting beach.
Tamarindo National Wildlife Refuge – Estuary and mangrove swamps.
Ostional National Wildlife Refuge – Turtle-nesting beach.
Isla del Coco National Park – Rainforest; coral reef; endemics.

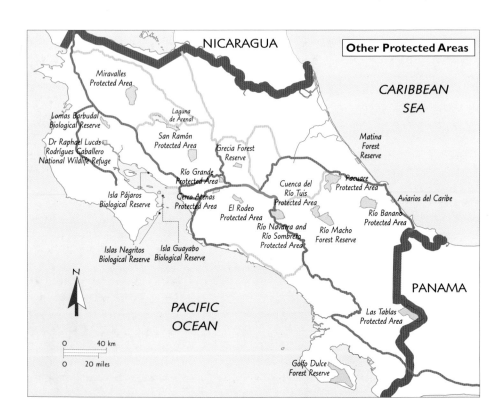

National Parks and Other Reserves

The South Nicoya/Tempisque Conservation Area
Barra Honda National Park – Limestone surface features; underground caves.
Palo Verde National Park – Wetlands; mangroves; saltwater lagoons; evergreen dry tropical forest.
Cabo Blanco Absolute Nature Reserve – Sea-bird nesting island; moist tropical forest.
Curú National Wildlife Refuge – Working hacienda; mangroves; turtle-nesting beach; dry tropical forest.
Other protected areas:
Lomas Barbudal Biological Reserve
Dr Raphael Lucas Rodrígues Caballero National Wildlife Refuge
Isla Pájaros Biological Reserve
Islas Negritas Biological Reserve
Isla Guayabo Biological Reserve

Central Pacific Conservation Area
Peñas Blancas Wildlife Refuge – Geological interest.
Carara National Park – Tropical moist forest; tropical wet forest; marshy flood plain.
Manuel Antonio National Park – Wet lowland rainforest; coastal features.
Marino Ballena National Park – Island with nesting sea birds; coral reef; offshore whales.

Osa Conservation Area
Isla del Caño Biological Reserve – Coral reef; lithic spheres.
Corcovado National Park – Lowland rainforest; mangrove swamps; tidal estuaries.
Piedras Blancas National Park – Primary evergreen rainforest.
Golfito National Wildlife Refuge – Evergreen rainforest.
Other protected area:
Golfo Dulce Forest Reserve

Central Volcanic Conservation Area
Volcán Irazú National Park – Volcanic features.
Volcán Poás National Park – Volcanic features.
Juan Castro Blanco National Park – Primary rain- and cloud forest.

Public Holidays and Festivals (Jul–Dec)

Mid-July – *Fiesta de la Virgen del Mar* (Feast of the Virgin of the Sea).
25 July – *Día de Guanacaste* (celebration of the annexation of Guancaste Province). Celebrates the province becoming part of Costa Rica.
2 August – *Día de la Virgen de los Ángeles* (Feast of Our Lady of the Angels, Patron Saint of Costa Rica).
15 August – Assumption of the Blessed Virgin. Also *Día de la Madre* (Mothers' Day).
15 September – Independence Day.
12 October – *Día de las Culturas* (Columbus Day).
Mid-October – Week-long Carnival in Puerto Limón.
25 December – Christmas Day (celebrations continue until 2 January).

National Parks Guide

Good Reading

Visitors interested in wildlife and birds will need good field guides: FC Stiles and AF Skutch (1989 with numerous reprints), *Guide to the Birds of Costa Rica*. Cornell University Press. The birder's bible. **Richard Garrigues and Robert Dean** (2007), *Birds of Costa Rica*. Helm Field Guides. Less bulky and more user friendly than the above guide, but not in so much detail. **Fogden, Susan CL** (2007), *Photographic Guide to Birds of Costa Rica*. Jadine Ediciones. Comprehensive pocket guide. **Philip de Vries** (1987), *The Butterflies of Costa Rica*. Princeton University Press. Comprehensive guide for lepidopterists. **Daniel H Janzen** (1983), *Costa Rican Natural History*. University of Chicago Press. For reference rather than field use. **Les Beletsky** (1998), *The Ecotravellers' Wildlife Guide*. Natural World Academic Press. Full coverage of the country's flora and fauna. General books include: **Richard, Karen and Mavis Biesanz** (1987), *The Costa Ricans*. Prentice Hall. Costa Rican politics and culture. **Barbara Ras** (Ed) (1994) *Costa Rica: A Traveller's Literary Companion*. Whereabouts Press. An English translation of 26 stories by Costa Rican writers.

Braulio Carrillo National Park – Rain- and cloud forest; volcanic features.
Lankester Botanical Gardens – Orchids, epiphytes and bromeliads.
Guayabo National Monument – Archaeological site; premontane forest.
Tenorio Volcano National Park – Volcanic features.
Turrialba Volcano National Park – Volcanic features.
Other protected areas:
Grecia Forest Reserve
Río Grande Protected Area
Cerro Atenas Protected Area
El Rodeo Protected Area

Highland Conservation Area

Tapantí National Park – Lower montane and premontane forest.
Chirripó National Park – Costa Rica's highest mountain; glacial features; páramo; mixed forest.
La Amistad International Park – Lowland rainforest; cloud forest; páramo.
Wilson Botanical Gardens (Los Cruces Biological Station) – Gardens of ornamental and tropical plants.
Other protected areas:
Las Tablas Protected Area
Río Navarra and Río Sombrero Protected Area
Cuenca del Río Tuis Protected Area
Río Macho Forest Reserve

Useful Websites

www.visitcostarica.com (official tourist board site)
www.sinac.go.cr (information on conservation areas and national parks)
www.costaricabureau.com (comprehensive information on hotels, reservations and tours)
www.costaricamap.com (general information and maps)
www.govisitcostarica.com (information on vacations, travel and hotels)
www.ticotimes.net (website of the English-language newspaper, useful for listings and current affairs)

Tourist Information

The **Costa Rican Tourist Board** (Instituto Costarriense de Turismo or ICT) is located below the Plaza de la Cultura, Avenida Central, Calle 3-5, San José, tel: 2223 1733. It also has an informative website (www.visitcostarica.com) and a desk at Juan Santamaría International Airport. It can supply accommodation details, city plans, maps and bus schedules. ICT offices outside of San José are rare, but many towns in Costa Rica have their own municipal tourist offices.

National Parks

The Costa Rican National Parks system is administered by **SINAC** (Sistema Nacional de Areas de Conservación), Apdo 10104, San José, tel: 2234 0973, www.sinac.go.cr For information contact the **Fundación de Parques Nacionales**, 300m north and 150m east of Santa Teresita Church, C 23, Av 15, Barrio Escalante, San José. You can pay in advance here for entrance to parks, but in most cases you can pay for entry at the ranger stations.

Tour Operators

Trips to Costa Rica can be arranged abroad through specialist Latin America tour operators. In the **USA**: **Costa Rica Experts**, 3166 N Lincoln Avenue, Suite 424, Chicago Il, tel: 1-800 827 0046, www.costaricaexperts.com Organized or off-the-shelf holidays arranged for all interests. **Holbrook Travel**, 3540 NW 13th Street, Gainesville Fl, 32609, 2196, tel: 800 451 7111, www.holbrooktravel.com Wide variety of tours organized. Holbrook own the Selva Verde Lodge near Puerto Viejo de Sarapiquí. In the **UK** try **Journey Latin America**, 12-13 Heathfield Terrace, Chiswick, London W4 4JE, tel: 020 8747 8315, www.journeylatinamerica.co.uk Specializes in cheap flights allied with bespoke wildlife and adventure tours.

Trips Worldwide, 14 Frederick Place, Clifton, Bristol BS8 1AS, tel: 0117 311 4400, www.tripsworldwide.co.uk Long established specialist in Latin American countries. Tailormade trips to Costa Rica for groups and individuals. **Voyages Jules Verne**, 21 Dorset Square, London NW1 6QG, tel: 020 7723 8629, www.vjv.co.uk They run a number of group tours to Costa Rica with the emphasis on wildlife and the option of a beachside extension. Ideal for the first-time visitor.

There are a huge number of San José-based tour operators, offering tours for adventure, wildlife, sport fishing, families, gays and weddings. The following have a proven record in providing group and bespoke wildlife tours and are licensed and regulated by the ICT: **Costa Rica Expeditions**, Apdo 6941, San José, tel: 2257 0766, www.costaricexpeditions.com The leader in the field, with wide experiences and resources, specializes in adventure and natural history tours either for groups or bespoke. Owns luxury lodges in Tortuguero and Monteverde and a tented camp in Corcovado. **Camino Travel**, PO Box 1049-2050, San Pedro, San José, tel: 2234 2530, www.caminotravel.com A young and enthusiastic group with a mainly European clientele. Organizes a wide range of tours, with tailor-made trips for groups and individuals. **TAM Travel C1**, Av Central/1, San José (and three other branches), tel: 2256 0203, www.tamtravel.com Professional organization dealing mainly with North American and up-market clients. **Costa Rica Trails**, PO Box 2907-100, San José, tel: 2803 3344, www.costaricantrails.com

Travel Tips

Well-established firm offering a variety of tours, with inspirational guides.

Money Matters

Currency: The central unit of currency in Costa Rica is the colon, plural colones, named after Christóbal Colón (Columbus) and divided into 100 céntimos. There are coins of 5, 10, 20, 25, 50, 100 and 500 colónes and notes of 50, 100, 500, 1000, 5000 and 10,000 colónes. Exchange rates with the dollar and pound sterling change regularly with inflation. Colónes are almost impossible to obtain abroad and visitors are advised to bring to Costa Rica a mixture of US$ travellers' cheques and US dollars, both of which are widely accepted.

Travellers' Cheques: buy these in US$ only. Travellers' cheques can only be used as cash in the higher-grade hotels. Cash and travellers' cheques are readily exchanged in banks and larger hotels, but be prepared for long waits in banks. Hotels will make a larger service charge than banks, but at least queues will be avoided.

Credit Cards: Visa and Mastercard widely accepted, AmEx less so. Smaller restaurants and hotels may only accept cash, although increasingly this will be rare. Most private banks will give an advance on credit cards. Many restaurants and shops add an additional charge to credit card transactions, which may be as high as 10%.

Banking Hours: Opening hours may vary slightly from branch to branch and region to region, but are usually Mon–Fri 09:00–15:00. Closed Sat. ATMs are found in most of the larger towns.

Taxes: There is a sales tax of 13% in restaurants, plus a service charge of 10%, which can be quite a shock when the bill arrives. Hotels charge 16.39%.

Business Hours

Offices are open 08:00–17:00 and shops and stores 09:00–18:00, but may close between noon and 14:00. Most shops open on Saturdays, but are closed on Sundays.

Public Holidays and Festivals

As Costa Rica is a Catholic country, many of the holidays are related to the church. On important holidays, hotels are likely to be fully booked. Government and business offices, banks and post offices are largely closed down from Christmas until the New Year and also during Easter Week.

Buses may not run during these times or operate a reduced service. Note also that bars are also closed from Thursday to Saturday during Holy Week and that they will also be closed on the days before and after a General Election.

Communications

The Costa Rican postal system, **Correos de Costa Rica**, is fairly efficient, but expect delays if posting mail from rural areas. Even small settlements will have a post office (*correo*) and a *lista de correo* or poste restante service, Although telephone calls within Costa Rica are cheap, long-distance calls can be expensive. The cheapest periods are between 20:00 and 07:00 and at weekends. The country code for Costa Rica is 506. All numbers have eight digits and there are no area codes. For information, dial 113, for international information call 124. Phone cards are widely used. There are a number of Internet cafés in San José, but few elsewhere in the country, although many hotels provide Internet access. Mobile phones usually connect with North America, but not with Europe. The English language newspaper, the *Tico Times*, is published weekly, with a daily online version.

Travel Tips

Time Difference

Costa Rica is six hours behind GMT and in North America's Standard time zone.

Electricity

The electrical supply is 110 volts, as in USA and Canada, with square pins. Visitors from Europe, Australia and other countries using 240 volts will need to have an adaptor.

Etiquette

It is natural in Costa Rican culture to be polite, friendly and responsible. *Ticos* like to leave a good impression. Dress tends to be formal, particularly in business situations. Shorts are out of place in San José and beachwear is not acceptable in churches. Both sexes tend to shake hands and men and women may kiss each other on the cheek. Saying hello and goodbye tends to take a long time. In line with their peaceful heritage, *Ticos* tend to avoid confrontation and if visitors have complaints they should make their point without putting a local person down. Make a point of praising them and their country – there is much to laud after all. The elderly are highly respected in Costa Rica – always use the prefix Don or Doña when referring to an older person.

The characteristic '*mañana* complex' prevalent in many Latin societies is not found in the Costa Rican tourist industry. Coach tours leave on time, as do private bus services, while appointments should be kept promptly. With regard to alcohol, although *Ticos* enjoy a drink, drunkenness is frowned upon. Drug possession is illegal and can result in a prison sentence.

Tipping

The American tipping culture seems to be gradually taking over in Costa Rica, but remember that restaurants automatically charge a 13% sales tax and a 10% service charge and most people would consider that this is sufficient without an extra tip. It is usual to give a small tip to hotel workers such as chambermaids and bellboys. Taxi drivers are not normally tipped. Tour guides, on the other hand, will often thoroughly deserve a little commission. Just remember that a tip should reflect the degree and quality of the personal service you have received.

Taking Home a Souvenir

One of the best momentos of Costa Rica is **coffee**. Café Britt is recognized as one of the best brands in the world and their products are available in gift shops and supermarkets, as well as at San José airport. Café Britt also produces a coffee liqueur along the lines of Kahlua. Costa Rica has a long tradition of **cigar** making – in fact many of the cigar makers in Cuba originally hailed from Costa Rica. Beware, however, of folk crafts, as many of the items on display in shops have been made elsewhere and imported into the country. Look out for genuine *indigenas items* such as the woven bags and baskets dyed by the Bribrí Indians and the carved balsa wood masks made by the Borucas. Inexpensive handmade jewellery and leather goods can also be found. A popular excursion is to the mountain village of Sarchí, known for the quality of its woodwork. Workshops can be visited where artisans can be seen making bowls, cutting boards, rocking chairs and gaily painted wooden ox carts. All the items can be packed and sent to your home address. Another genuine Costa Rican craft is the ceramic work made in villages in the Nicoya area of Guanacaste by the Chortega people. Eco-conscious tourists will wish to avoid buying coral and items made from turtle shell, furs or tropical hardwood.

Selected Animal and Bird Gallery

Jaguar

Jaguarundi

Ocelot

Margay

Baird's Tapir

Collared Peccary

Raccoon

Collared Anteater

Coati

Paca

Agouti

Common Opossum

Two-toed Sloth

Three-toed Sloth

Variegated Squirrel

White-tailed Deer

Spider Monkey

Leaf Cutter Ant

Howler Monkey

Red Brocket Deer

Bullet Ant

White-throated Capuchin

Squirrel Monkey

Zebra Longwing Butterfly

Blue Morpho Butterfly

Magnificent Owl Butterfly

Giant Swallowtail Butterfly

Animals

Green Sea Turtle

Loggerhead Sea Turtle

Olive Ridley Sea Turtle

Hawksbill Sea Turtle

Leatherback Sea Turtle

Caiman

Emerald Basilisk

American Crocodile

Green Iguana

Bushmaster

Jesus Christ Lizard

Gaudy Leaf Frog

Blue Jeans Dart Frog

Puffer fish

Fer-de-lance

Manta Ray

Humpback Whale

King Angelfish

Bigeye Jack

Bull Shark

Crocodile Needlefish

Rainbow Wrasse

Barracuda

Selected Animal and Bird Gallery

Black Vulture

Turkey Vulture

Common Black Hawk

Red-tailed Hawk

Roadside Hawk

Osprey

Laughing Falcon

Crested Caracara

White-winged Dove

Common Ground Dove

Black-cheeked Woodpecker

Hoffman's Woodpecker

Baird's Trogon

Slaty-billed Trogon

Great Kiskadee

Buff-throated Saltador

Lineated Woodpecker

Yellow-bellied Elaenia

Blue Gray Tanager

Crimson-collared Tanager

Summer Tanager

Birds

Chestnut-mandibled Toucan

Keel-billed Toucan

Red Lored Parrot

White crowned Parrot

Rufous-tailed Hummingbird

Magnificent Frigatebird

Resplendent Quetzal

Scarlet Macaw

Bananaquit

Chestnut-headed Oropendola

Montezuma's Oropendola

Groove-billed Ani

Tropical Gnatcatcher

Violet Sabrewing

Social Flycatcher

Red-winged Blackbird

Turquoise-browed Motmot

Tropical Kingbird

Purple Gallinule

Rufous-naped Wren

Selected Animal and Bird Gallery

Anhinga

Bare-throated
Tiger Heron

Black-crowned
Night Heron

Green Heron

Little Blue Heron

Glossy Ibis

Brown Pelican

Black-necked Stilt

Yellow-crowned
Night Heron

Jabiru

Northern Jacana

Olivaceous
Cormorant

White Ibis

Roseate
Spoonbill

Laughing Gull

Wood Stork

Belted Kingfisher

Green Kingfisher

Least Grebe

Royal Tern

Birds

Baltimore Oriole

Clay-coloured Robin

Bronze Cowbird

Ovenbird

Brown Booby

Great Egret

Cattle Egret

Grey-necked Wood-Rail

Blue and White Swallow

Barn Swallow

Snowy Egret

Great-tailed Grackle

Three-wattled Bellbird

Rufous-collared Sparrow

Prothonotary Warbler

White-throated Magpie-Jay

Brown Jay

Spotted Sandpiper

Collared Aracari

Check list

Top Mammals
- [ ] Agouti
- [ ] Baird's Tapir
- [ ] Coati
- [ ] Collared Anteater
- [ ] Collared Peccary
- [ ] Common Opossum
- [ ] Howler Monkey
- [ ] Jaguar
- [ ] Jaguarundi
- [ ] Margay
- [ ] Ocelot
- [ ] Paca
- [ ] Raccoon
- [ ] Red Brocket Deer
- [ ] Spider Monkey
- [ ] Squirrel Monkey
- [ ] Three-toed Sloth
- [ ] Two-toed Sloth
- [ ] Variegated Squirrel
- [ ] White-tailed Deer
- [ ] White-throated Capuchin

Top Reptiles
- [ ] American Crocodile
- [ ] Bushmaster
- [ ] Caiman
- [ ] Emerald Basilisk
- [ ] Fer-de-lance
- [ ] Green Iguana
- [ ] Green Sea Turtle
- [ ] Hawksbill Sea Turtle
- [ ] Jesus Christ Lizard
- [ ] Leatherback Sea Turtle
- [ ] Loggerhead Sea Turtle
- [ ] Olive Ridley Sea Turtle

Top Amphibians
- [ ] Blue Jeans Dart Frog
- [ ] Gaudy Leaf Frog

Top Insects
- [ ] Bullet Ant
- [ ] Leaf-cutter Ant
- [ ] Praying Mantis

Top Butterflies
- [ ] Blue Morpho
- [ ] Cydno Longwing
- [ ] Giant Swallowtail
- [ ] Magnificent Owl
- [ ] Monarch
- [ ] Zebra Longwing

Top Fish and Marine Mammals
- [ ] Barracuda
- [ ] Bigeye Jack
- [ ] Bull Shark
- [ ] Crocodile Needlefish
- [ ] Humpback Whale
- [ ] King Angelfish
- [ ] Manta Ray
- [ ] Puffer fish
- [ ] Rainbow Wrasse

Top Birds
- [ ] American Kestrel
- [ ] Anhinga
- [ ] Baird's Trogon
- [ ] Baltimore Oriole
- [ ] Bananaquit
- [ ] Bare-throated Tiger Heron
- [ ] Barn Swallow
- [ ] Barred Antshrike
- [ ] Belted Kingfisher
- [ ] Black-cheeked Woodpecker
- [ ] Black-crowned Night Heron
- [ ] Black-necked Stilt
- [ ] Black-shouldered Kite
- [ ] Black-tailed Whistling Duck
- [ ] Black Tern
- [ ] Black Vulture
- [ ] Blue and White Swallow
- [ ] Blue Gray Tanager
- [ ] Broad-winged Hawk
- [ ] Bronze Cowbird
- [ ] Brown Booby
- [ ] Brown Jay
- [ ] Brown Pelican
- [ ] Buff-throated Saltador
- [ ] Buff-throated Woodcreeper
- [ ] Cattle Egret

Check list

- ☐☐ Chestnut-headed Oropendola
- ☐☐ Chestnut-mandibled Toucan
- ☐☐ Clay-coloured Robin
- ☐☐ Collared Aracari
- ☐☐ Common Black Hawk
- ☐☐ Common Ground Dove
- ☐☐ Crested Caracara
- ☐☐ Crimson-collared Tanager
- ☐☐ Fasciated Tiger Heron
- ☐☐ Glossy Ibis
- ☐☐ Grey-necked Wood-Rail
- ☐☐ Great Blue Heron
- ☐☐ Great Egret
- ☐☐ Great Kiskadee
- ☐☐ Great-tailed Grackle
- ☐☐ Green Heron
- ☐☐ Green Ibis
- ☐☐ Green Kingfisher
- ☐☐ Groove-billed Ani
- ☐☐ Hoffman's Woodpecker
- ☐☐ House Sparrow
- ☐☐ Jabiru
- ☐☐ Keel-billed Toucan
- ☐☐ King Vulture
- ☐☐ Laughing Falcon
- ☐☐ Laughing Gull
- ☐☐ Least Grebe
- ☐☐ Lesser Yellowlegs
- ☐☐ Lineated Woodpecker
- ☐☐ Little Blue Heron
- ☐☐ Long-tailed Tyrant
- ☐☐ Magnificent Frigatebird
- ☐☐ Masked Booby
- ☐☐ Montezuma's Oropendola
- ☐☐ Mourning Dove
- ☐☐ Northern Jacana
- ☐☐ Olivaceous Cormorant
- ☐☐ Orange-fronted Parakeet
- ☐☐ Osprey
- ☐☐ Ovenbird
- ☐☐ Palm Tanager
- ☐☐ Prothonotary Warbler
- ☐☐ Purple Gallinule
- ☐☐ Red Lored Parrot
- ☐☐ Red-tailed Hawk
- ☐☐ Red-winged Blackbird
- ☐☐ Resplendent Quetzal
- ☐☐ Roadside Hawk
- ☐☐ Roseate Spoonbill
- ☐☐ Royal Tern
- ☐☐ Rufous-collared Sparrow
- ☐☐ Rufous naped Wren
- ☐☐ Rufous tailed Hummingbird
- ☐☐ Scarlet Macaw
- ☐☐ Scarlet-rumped Cacique
- ☐☐ Semipalmated Plover
- ☐☐ Short-billed Pigeon
- ☐☐ Slaty-billed Trogon
- ☐☐ Snowy Egret
- ☐☐ Social Flycatcher
- ☐☐ Spotted Sandpiper
- ☐☐ Summer Tanager
- ☐☐ Sunbittern
- ☐☐ Sun Grebe
- ☐☐ Three-wattled Bellbird
- ☐☐ Torrent Tyrannulet
- ☐☐ Tropical Gnatcatcher
- ☐☐ Tropical Kingbird
- ☐☐ Turkey Vulture
- ☐☐ Turquoise-browed Motmot
- ☐☐ Variable Seedeater
- ☐☐ Violet Sabrewing
- ☐☐ Whimbrel
- ☐☐ White-crowned Parrot
- ☐☐ White-fronted Parrot
- ☐☐ White Ibis
- ☐☐ White-throated Magpie-Jay
- ☐☐ White-winged Dove
- ☐☐ Willet
- ☐☐ Wood Stork
- ☐☐ Yellow-bellied Elaenia
- ☐☐ Yellow-billed Cacique
- ☐☐ Yellow-crowned Night Heron
- ☐☐ Yellow-faced Grassquit

Index

Index

Useful Phrases

English is widely spoken in the travel industry, but a few words in Spanish, the official language, will always be well received. Bring a phrase book and a Spanish dictionary. Spanish speakers should note that the informal *tu* is rarely used and the more formal *usted* is even used amongst friends and family. The following phrases may help:

Yes, No • *Sí, No*
Please • *Por favor*
Thank you • *Gracias*
Hello • *Hola*
Goodbye • *Adiós*
See you later • *Hasta luego*
My Name is ... • *Me llamo ...*
Do you speak English? • *¿Habla inglés?*
You're welcome • *De nada*

I don't speak Spanish • *No hablo español*
How much is ...? • *¿Cuánto cuesta ...?*
Do you have...? • *¿Tiene ...?*
Please speak more slowly • *Hable más despacio, por favor*
Where is ...? • *¿Donde está...?*
What time does it leave/arrive? • *¿A qué hora sale/llega?*

It's too expensive • *Es demasiado caro*
Do you have anything cheaper? • *¿No tiene algo más barato?*
Is there ...? • *¿Hay ...?*
Please fill the tank • *Llene el tanque, por favor*
Is there a hotel near here? • *¿Hay un hotel por aquí?*
Help! • *¡Ayúdeme!*

Imprint Page

First edition published in 2009
by New Holland Publishers (UK) Ltd
London • Cape Town • Sydney • Auckland
10 9 8 7 6 5 4 3 2 1
website: www.newhollandpublishers.com

Garfield House, 86 Edgware Road
London W2 2EA, United Kingdom

80 McKenzie Street
Cape Town 8001, South Africa

Unit 1, 66 Gibbes Street
Chatswood, NSW 2067, Australia

218 Lake Road, Northcote
Auckland, New Zealand

Distributed in the USA by
The Globe Pequot Press, Connecticut

ISBN 978 1 84773 134 0

This guidebook has been written by independent authors
and updaters. The information therein represents their
impartial opinion, and neither they nor the publishers
accept payment in return for including in the book or
writing more favourable reviews of any of the establishments. Whilst every effort has been made to ensure that
this guidebook is as accurate and up to date as possible,
please be aware that the facts quoted are subject to
change, particularly the price of food, transport and
accommodation. The Publisher accepts no responsibility
or liability for any loss, injury or inconvenience incurred
by readers or travellers using this guide.

Keep us Current
Information in travel guides is apt to change, which is
why we regularly update our guides. We'd be grateful to
receive feedback if you've noted something we should
include in our updates. If you have new information,
please share it with us by writing to the Publishing
Manager, Globetrotter, at the office nearest to you
(addresses on this page). The most significant contribu-
tion to each new edition will receive a free copy of the
updated guide.

Publishing Manager: Thea Grobbelaar
DTP Cartographic Manager: Genené Hart
Editor: Thea Grobbelaar
Design and DTP: Nicole Bannister
Cartographers: Tanja Spinola, Lorissa Bouwer,
Nicole Bannister
Picture Researchers: Shavonne Govender,
Zainoenisa Manuel
Consultant: Paul Murphy
Proofreader: Lorissa Bouwer
Illustrator: Steven Felmore

Reproduction by Resolution, Cape Town
Printed and bound in China by C & C Offset Printing
Co., Ltd.

Photographic credits:
jonarnoldimages.com: page 6 (centre); **John
Coletti/jonarnoldimages.com:** page 60; **Buddy
Mays:** title page, pages 27, 42 (bottom), 50 (top), 82
(centre), 96, 102 (bottom), 118, 133 (centre and
bottom); **Rowland Mead:** pages 6 (top), 13, 15,
114 (bottom), 122, 128, 142 (bottom); **Heather
Angel/Natural Visions:** pages 86, 100; **David
Cantrille/Natural Visions:** pages 41, 72 (top), 82
(bottom); **Richard Coomber/Natural Visions:**
half-title page, pages 50 (centre), 92 (bottom);
Richard Day/Natural Visions: page 77; **Brian
Rogers/Natural Visions:** pages 72 (centre), 92
(centre), 106; **Soames Summerhays/Natural
Visions:** page 36; **Ian Tait/Natural Visions:** pages
16, 82 (top); **Michael Windle/Natural Visions:**
page 62 (centre); **Papilio:** page 19; **Photo Access:**
pages 42 (top), 48, 62 (top), 62 (bottom), 136;
Nature Picture Library/Photo Access: front
cover, back cover (bottom), pages 7 (bottom), 32
(bottom), 59, 102 (top and centre), 111, 113, 114
(centre), 120, 133 (top), 142 (centre); **Fabio
Liverani/Nature Picture Library/Photo
Access:** page 69; **Lynn M. Stone/Nature Picture
Library/Photo Access:** page 142 (top); **Tom
Vezo/Nature Picture Library/Photo Access:**
page 71; **Sime/Photo Access:** page 72 (bottom);
Pictures Colour Library: contents page, pages 32
(top), 108; **Jeroen Snijders:** back cover (top and
centre), pages 24, 29, 32 (centre), 34, 42 (centre), 45,
50 (bottom), 64, 78, 92 (top), 114 (top), 126.

Front cover: *Unmistakable Scarlet Macaws, which may
be extending their range in Costa Rica.*
Back cover *(top to bottom):* One of the hundreds of
orchids on display at Lankester Gardens; a variety of egrets
and herons can be seen in the Tortuguero Channels;
Capuchin or White-faced Monkey, one of four monkey
species to be found in Costa Rica.*
Half title page: *The Squirrel Monkey is the smallest and
rarest of Costa Rica's four species of monkey.*
Title page: *The slow-moving Three-toed Sloth is common
in many of the low-lying areas of Costa Rica.*
Contents page: *The striking Chestnut-mandibled Toucan
can be found in the Caribbean and south Pacific lowlands.*